Advanced Information Technology
in the New Industrial Society

Advanced Information Technology in the New Industrial Society

THE KINGSTON SEMINARS

Edited by
ARTHUR COTTERELL

Principal, Kingston College
of Further Education
Kingston upon Thames, UK

Oxford   New York   Tokyo
OXFORD UNIVERSITY PRESS
1988

Oxford University Press, Walton Street, Oxford OX2 6DP

Oxford New York Toronto
Delhi Bombay Calcutta Madras Karachi
Petaling Jaya Singapore Hong Kong Tokyo
Nairobi Dar es Salaam Cape Town
Melbourne Auckland

and associated companies in
Berlin Ibadan

Oxford is a trade mark of Oxford University Press

Published in the United States
by Oxford University Press, New York

British Library Cataloguing in Publication Data
Advanced information technology in the new
industrial society: the Kingston seminars
1. Information systems. Technological
development I. Cotterell, Arther   001.5
ISBN 0–19–853285–7
ISBN 0--19–853290–3 Pbk

Library of Congress Cataloging in Publication Data
Advanced information technology in the new industrial society: the
Kingston Seminars/edited by Arthur Cotterell.
p. cm. 'The inaugural Kingston Seminars on Advanced Information
Technology, jointly sponsored by Lever Brothers and Kingston College
of Further Education . . . 1986'—Introd.
Bibliography: p.
1. Information technology—Economic aspects—Great Britain—
Congresses. 2. Information technology—Social aspects—Great
Britain—Congresses. 3 Industry and education—Great Britain—
Congresses. I. Cotterell, Arthur. II. Kingston Seminars on
Advanced Information Technology (1986) III. Lever Brothers Ltd.
IV. Kingston College of Further Education.
HC260.I55A38 1988   338.4'7004'0941—dc 19   87-34878 CIP
ISBN 0–19–853285–7
ISBN 0–19–853290–3 (pbk.)

Typeset by Joshua Associates Limited, Oxford
Printed in Great Britain
at the University Printing House, Oxford
by David Stanford
Printer to the University

Foreword

ROBERT McLOY
Director of Education and Recreation, Royal Borough of
Kingston upon Thames

It is a time-honoured practice to bestow particular theme titles upon particular years. For the administrator receiving exhortations about such initiatives it is not always welcomed. There is a sense in which it conveys a signal that 'they' wish to change the world, but without providing extra resources. All will be done simply by a re-direction of internal energies. Whose energies? Not theirs, but ours. This is hyperbole, but I suspect that many in the education world initially confessed to such sentiments about the designation of Industry Year. Nevertheless, such has been the response of the education service overall, that even the doubters must be persuaded that it is an initiative that has done much good.

The publicity surrounding Industry Year, as much as the many events that have been promoted under its umbrella, has effectively underlined our current near desperate plight. There can be few now who cannot be seriously concerned about the prospects for our economy when the supply of North Sea oil effectively dries up. There is a general recognition within the education world that more must be done, since an insufficient number of technologists and technicians are being trained and entering industry. As a consequence, our earning capacity as a nation is falling sharply. More must be done to stimulate the interest of young people (and their parents) in design, engineering, and information technology so that significantly larger numbers of well motivated and properly prepared people enter industry.

On a personal basis, there was no moment of dramatic conversion, though I do confess that I left a meeting in Whitehall, to which I and other Chief Education Officers had been summoned, quite shaken by the presentation of estimates relating to our rather gloomy prospects for economic growth. Most present had concluded that immediate action was called for and I doubt whether I was alone in having considerable worries as to whether everything possible had been done in my sphere. However, in Kingston upon Thames many initiatives took place to enhance the aims of Industry Year. Following one particular workshop session it was proposed to undertake research aimed at addressing the urgent task. Subject to detailed planning, it was envisaged that the initiative would include:

(1) heightening the general awareness of the problem and opportunities;

(2) identifying disincentives in the education system (very few girls enter engineering) and remedial steps;

(3) intensifying career guidance in this field;

(4) effecting better continuity between the stages of education and subsequent employment;

(5) establishing creative incentives to stimulate interest in careers in design, engineering and information technology.

The project, initially to last 3 years, would involve Kingston Polytechnic, Kingston College of Further Education, local schools, the careers service, companies, and parents.

Industry Year has provided a platform for debate and action. The programme of seminars on Advanced Information Technology, energetically promoted by Kingston College of Further Education in collaboration with Lever Brothers, is an example of what can and is being achieved. Here we witness a lively partnership between industry and education, focused at the critically important stage of further education and training. Industry Year is about partnership: the growing together in understanding between the worlds of learning and employment. With passion and commitment from all of these sources we can and will build a better and more prosperous society.

Acknowledgements

I should like to thank all the speakers at the Kingston Seminars for their generous donations of time and knowledge. Those in the audience certainly found the concern they expressed for the appropriate application of Information Technology encouraging. In Kingston, thanks are also due at Lever Brothers to Victor Rice-Smith and Bill Donnelly for making the series possible, and at the College to Jonathan Briggs, Richard Ennals, Paul French, Sue Holden, and Celia Walker for invaluable help with the seminar arrangements and transcripts afterwards. I am also indebted to Robert McCloy for his foreword and Paul Brodie for his chairmanship of the six seminars.

Kingston upon Thames   A.C.
1987

Contributors

Professor Igor Aleksander is Head of the Kobler Unit for IT Management at Imperial College of Science and Technology:

Sir Geoffrey Allen FRS is Director of Research and Engineering for Unilever plc.

Derek Barker is Manager of the IT Research Unit of British Petroleum at Sunbury.

Arthur Cotterell is Principal of Kingston College of Further Education.

Chris Humphries is Assistant Director of the Council for Educational Technology for the United Kingdom.

Bill Jordan is President of the Amalgamated Engineering Union.

Brian Oakley is Director of the Alvey Research Programme.

Dave Rogers is National Officer of the Electrical Electronic Telecommunications & Plumbing Union.

Derek Seddon is Director of Information Technology for the Imperial Chemical Industries plc.

Dr John Taylor is Director of the Research Centre of Hewlett Packard Laboratories at Bristol.

Contents

Introduction

ARTHUR COTTERELL

General awareness of the key role Information Technology (IT) will play in future economic development in Britain dates from the 1982 report of the Alvey Committee. Essentially a response to Japan's Fifth Generation Computer Programme, the recommendations of the Alvey Committee on Advanced Information Technology led to the establishment of a £350 million national research programme, a collaborative effort between industry, education, and research organizations, with companies paying half the costs of their involvement.

The Alvey initiative has been less focused than the Japanese programme, with sections of the Alvey Directorate concerned with the enabling technologies of Man–Machine Interface, Intelligent Knowledge-Based Systems, Software Engineering and Very Large Scale Integration. A further extension in 1984 addressed Declarative Systems Architectures, supporting work on parallel computer architectures, logic programming, and large data bases.

The market value of Information Technology in 1980 was £55 000 million in the West, whereas the total for 1990 is estimated at £150 000 million. The UK market share is approximately 5 per cent or about £4000 million this year. The Japanese estimate their current share of the market is 15 per cent and will be 40 per cent in 1990.

A key factor overlooked in the haste to respond to the Japanese challenge was technician training. No mention was made in the Alvey report of the role that further education institutions could play in the crucial area of technology transfer. Concern was, however, expressed about the uncontrolled spread of microcomputers accompanied by a poor understanding of BASIC. It was stated that the provision of hardware in schools was not enough, for 'teachers must be properly trained, and the languages taught chosen with an eye to the future'. Admission though this is of the inadequacy of conventional 'computer literacy', it understates the fundamental educational issue; namely, that in the context of fifth generation computers such a limited and limiting impression of the power of new technology could prove nationally disastrous. For the principal problem today of both education and training is not so much money or the lack of equipment, despite the difficulties these obviously cause, but rather a serious shortfall of 'high-technology manpower', of people who have learnt to think well in an environment of high technology. Indeed, the question of the technician skills which will be required for the era of fifth generation computing remains largely unconsidered.

The Cabinet Office paper *Learning to Live with IT* (1986) recognized that something would have to be done in order to adjust the education system to the onrush of new technology, not least because the school population of today is the workforce of the year 2000, but so far a national policy has not been formulated. There is still no programme for research and development into Information Technology in education and training, or into Information Technology's effect on both of them. This must be regarded as a missed opportunity, given the head-start Chris Humphreys suggests that the United Kingdom has in the application of high-technology to learning (Chapter 2). He sees our flexibility and practicality as positive assets in a field often preoccupied with hype. Further funds, on a continuing basis, are clearly needed for IT-based applications in schools, colleges, and universities in order to maintain the momentum of investment already made in Information Technology. They are urgently required so that we can ascertain the scope of the opportunities available as well as the nature of the inevitable limitations of IT-based learning. The Cabinet Office paper was surely correct too in arguing for the acceleration of development work in a small number of educational establishments through special grants.

Where a fascinating interface between the formal education system, and industry and commerce is already becoming apparent is in the experience of day-release students at colleges of further education and in the further education experience of trainees on the Youth Training Scheme. Because these young people are often exposed to the latest applications of new technology at work, their expectations of curriculum content and approach tend to be less constrained by tradition. It is not entirely surprising, therefore, that in colleges of further education the implications of fifth generation computers are now beginning to receive serious attention.

Kingston College of Further Education is a case in point. With the aid of a Nuffield Foundation award an IT Development Unit was set up in 1985, its brief to relate fifth generation computing to post-compulsory education and training as a whole. Specifically, the Unit is charged with the development of a core introductory course for all students and the application of Expert Systems to learning problems identified within both the further education curriculum and the field of company-based training. Working with Expert Systems environments across such a wide spectrum—from CNC milling and hairdressing treatments at one extreme to financial modelling and cell identification at another—has not only persuaded staff and students that logic programming is an aid to clearer thinking, but even more it has brought about a realization that there is much common ground between the development activities of companies and colleges. As Chris Tompsett, the head of the IT Development Unit, remarked of the Expert System,

... the potential to have help available when required, rather than when provided by the expert, the freedom from the continual need to be immersed in manuals on the latest machine and the provision of embedded training—training as an integral element in the computer system—will all free the technician to tackle a task with increased flexibility, greater assurance and in a fashion that places increasing emphasis on understanding alongside skill.

An industrial example of this kind of advance is given by John Taylor (Chapter 4). It concerns the use of computer imagery for fault finding in an oil refinery. He points out that when an Expert System capable of giving advice according to the characteristics of a flame is involved, then remedial action can be taken as soon as a difficulty arises. However, the expertise deployed in the system needs to be easy to use and constantly updated, not least because technology and knowledge are changing at a colossal rate. Equally cautious about the information to be used is Sir Geoffrey Allen, who argues that its quality is only as good as the thought that went into its selection (Chapter 3).

If Advanced Information Technology, as instanced in the oil industry, is to support and strengthen the fabric of industrial society it must form part of a general political, social, and economic debate. It has to be placed in a wider context than the profits of a single company. Because we are so adaptable we hardly notice how new technology increasingly transforms our lives. A glance at the chart below will show the advances made over the last 50 years.

For the young the pace of change is already a fact of everyday life. They find nothing extraordinary in the advent of the microcomputer, at home or in school. For adults the transformation is more

	1940s	1950s	1960s	1970s	1980s
Microelectronics	Valves	Transistors	Integrated Circuits	LSI	VLSI
Computers	Special purpose	Mainframes	Minis	Micros Supercomputers	PC's Superminis
Software	Machine Code	FORTRAN COBOL	Time-share OS ALGOL	DBMS LISP	PROLOG ADA
Communications	Strowger Radio-telegraph	Crossbar Microwave FDM	Stored program Satellite TDM	Digital Switching & Transmission Fibre Packet	

Fig. i.1 Information Technology: accelerating change.

problematic, especially when new technology goes hand in hand with unemployment. As Bill Jordan says of trade unionists (Chapter 5),

... we see Information Technology in particular fuelling the pace of change to the point of it taking on the characteristics of a nuclear chain reaction, with all the same potential for benefiting society if uncontrolled, or causing considerable damage to the stability of society and to individuals within it if unchecked.

The far-reaching implications of what can only be called the New Technology Industrial Revolution must be faced by the management of large and small companies, and by their workforces and trades unions. They must also lie at the core of education, training, and research for the new industrial society in which we shall all have to live. Fortunately, Advanced Information Technology can in itself offer a new medium for communication and the exchange of knowledge within the community, although as Professor Aleksander notes (Chapter 6),

... technological change must only be used to allow people to do what they always wanted to do ... A part of our national problem is that many managers do not know what they want to do.

If this publication encourages further thought about the near-future impact of fifth generation computers and stimulates much needed discussion about national priorities, then I am sure that both contributors and sponsors will be satisfied. Printed here are addresses given in the autumn of 1986 by distinguished speakers to an invited audience of industrialists, educationalists, scientists, public administrators, and journalists. The series constituted the inaugural Kingston Seminars on Advanced Information Technology, jointly sponsored by Lever Brothers and Kingston College of Further Education as part of Industry Year 1986. Since the report of the Bide Committee was published shortly after the last seminar, some of its recommendations for Information Technology policy are presented in the appendix.

1 An overview of research and co-operation in Advanced Information Technology

BRIAN OAKLEY

The only reason, I think, that I am Director of the Alvey Programme is that I am the only person who has worked for the Department of Industry, the Ministry of Defence, and the Science Research Council, and survived. The subject of Advanced Information Technology is vital to our society and is going to be of immense importance to the future of this and any other country.

Inexorably, year after year, the value of the market for Information Technology grows, and the overall trend is clear. In the last year there has been a significant decline in the market for integrated circuits, but this should be seen as short term. The Japanese share of the market is 15 per cent, a remarkable achievement when you consider their position a few years ago. There are signs, however, that they are having great difficulty in making major inroads into the market except in certain specialist areas, such as semiconductors and peripherals. In the field in which I am most interested, in the new applications of Information Technology, Artificial Intelligence, and Software Technology, they have yet to make their mark in the world market.

Historical perspectives

The great growth in the industry has taken place because of three very obvious technological breakthroughs, where costs have fallen dramatically: in communications, computer storage, and computer power. You may remember the prediction that was made when Univac, the first commercial computer, came to the market and IBM, a firm that made mechanical machines such as desk calculators, were asked if they were interested. After a market survey they concluded that five of these machines would satisfy all of the known needs of the United States, so they delayed. It was not until the

'Whirlwind' project that the position changed, and defence requirements produced a market for computers for IBM. Two hundred
Whirlwind computers were bought by the Americans at the time of
the Korean War, which helped to establish IBM on its current
course. Without major technological breakthroughs, the market
would not have expanded in the way that it has.

Communications

I do not think that we realize the extent of the revolution through
which we are living. We are all accustomed to a telephone with a
band width and information capacity of something like 10 kHz. The
twisted pair of wires that runs into the telephone could perhaps carry
10 kHz over any reasonable distance. Cities like Swindon are being
recabled with co-axial cable which would give you a band width
perhaps a thousand times greater, with a cable which is no bigger.
Fibre optics are now becoming available, thanks in no small part to
the technological genius of this country, and they offer a capacity at
least a million times that of the telephone line. That means you can
have the equivalent of a million telephones on your desk instead of
one. We must realize that for the same cost, in fact for ever declining
cost, we can get this enormous increase in capacity.

It may be, of course, that the data base which we and our children
use may not be in London, but in New York or Tokyo. The cost of
communication will become negligible compared with the cost of
extracting and storing the data. The first trans-ocean fibre optic
cable is being laid across the English Channel and the first trans-
Atlantic cable, in an advanced stage of planning, is due to go into
service in 1988 followed by three others. There is sudden competition and the prospect of a surplus of capacity across the Atlantic for
the first time. It is likely that the costs will continue to fall and that the
impact will be wider than for the revolution in computing.

Computer storage

Cheap computer power is almost entirely due to cheap integrated
circuits. We have not noticed cheaper computer storage as a
separate development because it has been part of the overall
computer revolution. In some of my early papers I predicted the
amount of computer storage which would be required to run some of
the air traffic control systems and so on in this country; these are the
sort of storage capacities we now expect on a home computer.

We are now seeing the impact of cheap peripheral devices. The use of optical discs will lead to much the same mechanical, electro-mechanical equipment for peripheral storage, but with a capacity roughly a thousand times greater for no increase in cost, which again revolutionalizes the way we think about stored data.

The reason that these developments have occurred is to a very large extent due to what has happened on chips, on integrated circuits. There is a law, known as 'Moore's Law', that says that the complexity of the chip doubles every year. It certainly conforms with recent experience. We have had to make the resolution, the amount of information we put onto the chip, smaller and smaller in order to comply with that law. The reason for that is that we are working with wafers of silicon, which are divided up into little squares, perhaps a centimetre square, which form the integrated circuits. When you consider the inevitable impurities in the silicon, it is clear that the smaller the rectangle of the circuit, the higher the yield, the higher the probability is that the square will not actually contain an impurity. We have also reached the point where the actual switching speed of the circuit on the surface of the silicon is no longer important compared with the time of the electrons moving between the switches on the surface and therefore, if you want to go faster, you have to make smaller and smaller circuits (Figs 1.1 and 1.2).

We are now working with something approaching 256 k per chip, the standard chip you can now buy for your microcomputer. One-megabit chips will be commercially available soon. Following Moore's Law we can predict 4-megabit chips by the early 1990s. To reach this stage we have had to work with line widths on the chips of about a micron, a hundredth of the width of a human hair. We cannot expect to get much below 0.3 microns, as the lines will be becoming so thin, with only a few tens of atoms across the lines (Figs 1.3 and 1.4). The difficulty of working at these levels is that the wavelength of light is roughly comparable to 1 micron, so we have to make use of X-rays or electron beams, which has of course placed a great strain on research capabilities as high energy physics is put to industrial use. In principle the production of integrated circuits is not unlike that of running off prints of your photographs once the negative has been produced. If you make enough of them, they become negligibly cheap. Your design costs can be written off against a large produc-tion run.

Each of these memory chips in turn has dropped in price until you pay about the same price for a chip, whatever the memory. Indeed,

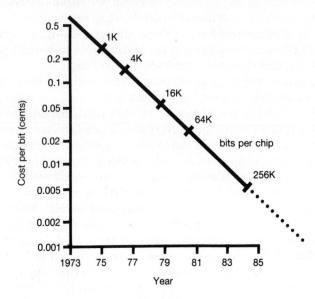

Fig. 1.1 IC memory costs per bit.

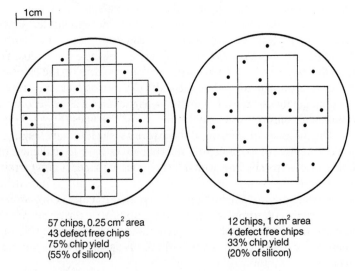

57 chips, 0.25 cm² area
43 defect free chips
75% chip yield
(55% of silicon)

12 chips, 1 cm² area
4 defect free chips
33% chip yield
(20% of silicon)

Fig. 1.2 Improving the yield of chips from silicon.

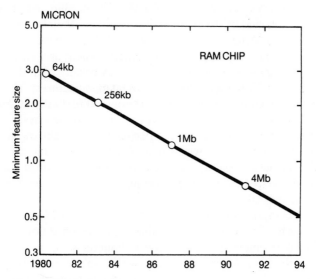

Fig. 1.3 Increasing bit size.

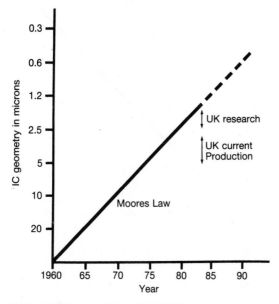

Fig. 1.4 Integrated circuit geometry.

last year you actually paid less for the 256-k chip, which was probably explained by the claim of the Americans that the Japanese were dumping. America, like the UK (with the sole exception of Philips), lost out very largely on the entertainment and electronic business to Japan, and the Americans are extremely keen that this should not happen to their integrated circuit manufacturers. There is no question that the Japanese entered the market first with the 256-k chip and are now well ahead of the Americans in some ways.

However, the Americans are determined to regain the major portion of the market. They saw that after the 256-k chip the next stage would be 1 megabit, and decided to jump that stage and go straight ahead to 4 megabits, and get ahead of the Japanese. What are the Japanese doing?

Just to complete the story let me tell you that, if Moore's Law really does hold, by the year 2000 we will have reached down to the twelve active elements per chip which is about the same number as a neuron in the brain. My one prediction with absolute certainty is that by then we will discover there are a lot more neurons in the brain. (Fig. 1.5).

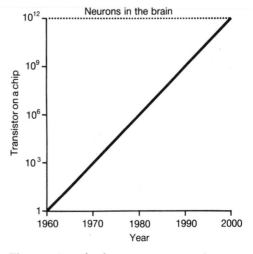

Fig. 1.5 Growth of components on a chip.

Computer power

If you plot the power of computers at the time of their introduction, you can see that the power of computers has gone up by a factor of

10, roughly every 6 years or so. My favourite was Atlas: the last time that the United Kingdom held the Blue Riband for computer power. Some of you in the business will remember that IBM came along and inspected the Atlas very shortly after, and learnt a few useful lessons. The BBC micro is not really very much less powerful than the Atlas which filled a large room. Unfortunately, the amount of power we are getting is actually not enough for what we are trying to do. This may seem extraordinary, but the fact is that the form of computing that we are going into now, inference computing, is enormously expensive on computer power and we need more. Somehow, we are going to have to speed up that curve, if we are going to get the developments we are talking about.

I must digress for a moment and say something about chess. You will remember that with great relief at the end of the war, scientists stopped playing about with predicting the accuracy of bombs, where they ought to put them, and so on, and turned to playing nice chess games with computers. It took them a few months to put in the rules of chess because there really are not all that number of rules for 64 squares on a chess board (actually there are 70 rules). It comes as a bit of a surprise to discover that there are that number, but those are really the edge conditions, the boundary conditions, and so on. Having got the rules in then you clearly just run the computer until you have found the optimum solution, the particular position that the board shows and there is the answer—easy to do. It was at that point that they discovered that there were actually $10^{15\,790}$ possible chess games and even with the sort of power that our computers have got today, that does take just a little time. That is known as the combinational explosion and for those of you who cannot really imagine what that number is like, I am told there are 10^{18} seconds since the earth was formed. It shows that we are dealing with really quite a large number.

I have cheated a bit in this argument, and I have insulted all my friends in the Artificial Intelligence world, but it is a clear indication of the problems that we face as we go into the sort of computing where one is likely to have to search through a whole tree of possible answers in order to find the optimum route—the combinational explosion. Essentially, the Artificial Intelligence community, ever since then, has been finding ways of tricking that explosion, of cutting out branches of the trees, of jumping to conclusions, and so on.

Incidentally, it is interesting that we older scientists, were taught at that time that science worked by the Baconian process: you carry out an experiment, look at the result, and deduce from the results what the law must be. That is forward treeing in an inference sense. We now know that it is not true at all. What actually happens is that the scientist proposes his hypothesis and then experiments in order to prove or disprove his assumption. That is backward treeing; it is what you do when you come to your car and it will not start, and after kicking it, you think for a while, you decide what the possible solution is, and you fiddle about and see whether that solution is right. It is all a method of avoiding the enormous tree which you would have if you logically worked through the whole process.

Technological challenges

At this point I think I can summarize what the technological challenges are that we face, if the explosion in information technology is destined to carry on. They are VLSI, parallel computing, inference computing, and speech and image recognition. Additionally, there is natural language understanding.

VLSI (Very Large Scale Integration) is integrated circuit development, where wafer scale integration is actually building bigger and bigger circuits. You can see that the problem of reliability comes in there because of the impurities I referred to.

Parallel computing is a challenge because the only obvious way of speeding up the process of getting more and more computing power is to have a whole lot of computers in parallel, and I do not just mean 10 or 100. We have reached the point now where we have a computer on a chip; if you make enough of them, they become dirt cheap, so why not have many computers in parallel. Indeed, the next generation of microcomputers that children play with will have many computers in parallel on it, no doubt. There are some minor problems, because we are actually talking about an enormous array of computers in certain cases. The biggest actual project I know is aimed at having a million such computers in a large array. You can see the sort of applications where it would really fit rather well. The chess game that I referred to just now: supposing you had 64, one for each square, you can see the way it would speed up the game. In fact there is just such a machine: it is known as Belle, compared sometimes with the world chess champions. It does not always win: last year it lost out to a Cray machine, the reason being that the Cray team spotted that the Belle team was frantically programming at the end game of the Belle so they concentrated on the end game and sure enough they won. It is always rather comforting to know that computers are not infallible. Incidentally, I will leave it to you to guess which laboratory actually produces Belle.

Inference computing is a whole new field that is opening up. If the other branches of computing have grown fast, then it is my belief that once we actually get onto the growth curve in a big way, we shall find that inference computing becomes enormously important in virtually every walk of life. The reason why I make that prediction is simply this; the sort of computing which we have used up to now is really based on the laws of arithmetic and on Boolean algebra. By and large, what we use computers for is doing mathematics, although we may do simple sorting and so on. However, if you actually think about the decisions you make in your life, the vast majority of them are not really based on mathematics in that sense.

They are actually based on inferring what to do from an uncertain set of rules which you have built up in your mind over your working life, on probably inaccurate or incomplete data. The rules themselves are probably contradictory and uncertain, and so on. It is a whole new field we are entering into, characterized by Expert Systems (Fig. 1.6), which can provide assistance with solving

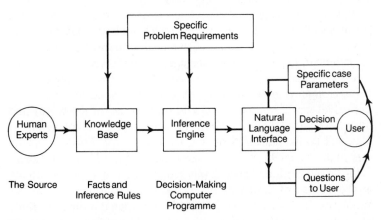

Fig. 1.6 Expert Systems.

problems in well-understood knowledge areas. There has been a growing number of commercial applications in the past decade, with the lead taken by laboratories in the United States, using powerful computer workstations.

Speech and image recognition are now developing rapidly. I have seen a speech recognizer, working in real time, in operation in Yorktown Heights, the laboratory of IBM in the United States (one of the most advanced computing laboratories in the world). We have been playing about with speech recognition for a very long time, but because of the combinational explosion, the actual process of searching back through the tree to assemble and make sense of the sentence, which you really have to do if you are going to carry out speech recognition with an acceptable degree of accuracy, is so difficult and consumes so much time that it was really not possible, until very recently, to actually do it in real time. It is now reaching the point where you can dictate to your computer. The errors will still be there, but you are sure to have a process of getting immediate feedback on the screen and correcting the errors. The reason why I found this so exciting was that you could see the sentence coming up on the screen as the operator said the words and, as the sentence built up, so the machine was learning more about what the sentence was all about and therefore deducing back, to correct the early words in the sentence.

Image recognition has applications in fields such as robots with visual functions and medical diagnosis.

Natural Language Understanding remains a problem. We have learnt now that, with the exception of very small vocabularies, there is little chance really of valid speech recognition without a great deal of understanding of natural language, our understanding what the whole sentence is about. We would need to understand the context, because that is how we work. We do not actually hear every individual word, but we actually listen to a few of the words and interpret what all the rest is about. Let me just give a simple example. You will know that the former Lord Chancellor, Lord Hailsham, was really rather keen on the ceremonial of the House of Lords, being an old fashioned peer. It was actually quite an experience to be in the House of Lords at 3 o'clock when he processed to the Woolsack. If you are in the House of Lords then it is the done thing to go out and line the corridors as the Lord Chancellor goes past. As Lord Hailsham was progressing through the hall one day, he saw one of his friends in a crowd and he called out 'Neil' and all the American visitors got down on their knees.

Let me just give one more example of this very difficult subject of natural language that we are entering. Let us accept that we are going to have a greater understanding of what the structure of language is, of the way in which we create sentences; the way in which we understand sentences, in fact an understanding of the extraordinary phenomenon that speech is. The more we look at it, the more we realize how clever we human beings are. Even 3-year-old children can still cope with language far better than all the Artificial Intelligence experts in the world can cope using their computers. Let me give an example of the natural language problem: supposing you taught a computer to understand the sentence; 'time flies like an arrow'. It is a perfectly reasonable sentence; it has a verb and should be a perfectly reasonable thing for a computer to understand. Of course, it is a slightly poetic type of sentence, but none of us have the slightest difficulty in inderstanding what it means. Shakespeare, I suppose, wrote it originally: it has now become something which none of us would have any real difficulty in understanding and you could teach a computer to parse that sentence, to recognize what each of the words were, and perhaps extract the meaning out of it. Having done that of course, the next sentence the computer comes across is 'fruit flies like an apple'. Well, I leave you to mull over the small difficulties that arise at that point.

There are numerous examples of this type. None of us have any problems with them, but I can assure you that it really is very difficult to actually get computers to the point where they can cope. It restores one's faith in human beings.

Knowledge-based systems

Let me say a word about knowledge-based systems because they are so important; this is the large new growth area. When one creates a knowledge-base, or, if you like, a rule base, one says to the expert whose knowledge one is trying to represent: 'how do you make these decisions?' Out of that you extract some rules, put them in a rule base, and then you have to have an inference engine which is essentially a computer optimized for doing the sort of tree-searching that I was talking about. You feed in the particular parameters of the situation you are dealing with, and then out comes an answer. However, there are two major problems.

1. It is really very difficult to put the knowledge base together, extracting the knowledge, classifying it, and making it in a regular form which minimizes the amount of searching required. A story I like—a true story—concerns DEC's experience with a program known as R1 (now known as XCON). DEC, the Digital Electronics

Corporation, decided that they would set out to build an Expert System. They decided to omit these ambitious professional Expert Systems, which of course the academics all went for (medical Expert Systems and so on) which naturally are about as difficult as you can make Expert Systems because after all they are intended to save us from paying the fabulous fees we pay for our medical specialists. DEC went to Carnegie–Mellon University and asked whether it was possible to build an expert system to configure computers: a very elementary operation which quite a lowly operator or technician does. The task is actually buying his machine: he fills out a form and sends it off, and then somebody gets all the parts together and sends them off. Anybody who has ever been concerned with installing a computer will know that one can be absolutely certain that something will be wrong in the kit of parts that actually comes to you. The cable will either be too short or you will have one of the peripherals wrong or something like that. Nevertheless, it is essentially a straight store-keeping operation.

Carnegie–Mellon University said it ought to be perfectly possible. They carried out experiments for 6 months, at the end of which time they had done enough work for the DEC management to be convinced that it was actually worthwhile carrying on and developing an Expert System to carry out this operation. So they worked hard with these experts, the technicians, for a couple of years, and at the end of that time, they had extracted from the experts all the knowledge that they had about how they actually configured. They had about 2000 rules of the rule base. They then went back to DEC and said, 'right, done, let us use it and go live'. They used it; now, 2 years after that, the number of rules has doubled from 2000 to 4000. The experts did not realize just how clever they were; they were not able to put over the degree of expertise they had got.

2. I am also seriously concerned with the output of Expert Systems because I think we are going to have many problems where we have really got to be very careful and be on our guard. The reason why the problem arises is that, on the whole, if you ask a computer to solve an arithmetical problem it will give an answer which we all treat as correct. Those of us who use computers professionally for analysis or some computer operations where enormous precision is required, know all the dangers or rounding errors and so on, but basically we all know that when we ask a computer to add two and two, it will of course get the answer, 3.9999 . . . and so on. We treat it as correct. However, if you have inference computing, you cannot

expect the answer that you get to be necessarily correct because the rule base is sure to be incomplete and may well be contradictory. The actual requirement of the problem, the particular data you are getting in, will be uncertain and may be itself contradictory. So, what you actually get out is the best inference that the machine is able to make on the rules that it has and the data that is fed in. There is a probability that the program will produce an incorrect answer. That does not mean to say that Expert Systems are not enormously valuable, but it does mean that we have got to be very careful that we do not fall into the trap of believing that they are always going to be right. It means that we have got to learn to use them. Some people say that an Expert System should by law, be required to produce two answers, with the associated probabilities. If one did that, then I think one would be in a much safer position when judging whether the advice that has been offered is good or not.

Notice, incidentally, that we have long passed the point of believing that Expert Systems are going to replace the human experts. They are going to supplement and help them. I think you have only got to realize that if a doctor meets a case which he has learnt about in his education in medical school 40 years ago, but has never met since, there is a pretty fair chance that he has forgotten all about it and will not recognize what it is, but with a computer, if the data is put in once, then on the whole the computer will not forget.

The economics of information technology

At this point I am going to turn to the consideration of the economics of the industry and in particular of the industry that Britain faces.

It is interesting to look at a table of the electronics firms of Europe (Table 1.1). You can pick out the British ones (italicized), and you will see that the UK is well represented, scattered throughout the table. It is when you actually come to look at the situation of the league table of the world that you begin to get rather more worried. Table 1.2 shows the top 20 electronic firms of the world and you will notice that the UK only figures once in that table. GEC is in fifteenth place. If you look at the turnover of IBM, almost $46 billions in 1984, compared with GEC's $6 billions, you can see that we really are pigmies in a giants' game.

Let us look in slightly more detail at one which has been in the news recently—the telecommunications industry. At first sight, if you look at Table 1.3, it looks reasonably satisfactory. In Western

Table 1.1 The electronics firms of Euorpe (1985)

Ranking 1985	Company	Country	Market capital ($m)	Turnover Ranking	Turnover this year ($m)	Employees
1	BT	UK	16 363	—	9 798	238 304
2	Siemens	GER	8 942	2	14 958	319 000
3	General Electric	UK	5 650	3	6 146	127 460
4	Philips	NET	3 267	1	15 581	344 000
5	Cable and Wireless	UK	2 996	—	1 103	24 016
6	Telefonica	SPA	2 360	—	1 793	66 781
7	Ericsson LM	SWE	1 202	8	3 318	75 116
8	Plessey	UK	1 151	11	1 812	37 553
9	Olivetti	ITA	1 138	10	2 344	47 613
10	Racal Electronics	UK	1 051	15	1 417	25 220
11	Thorn EMI	UK	973	4	4 102	90 327
12	STC	UK	937	9	2 518	52 218
13	Electrolux	SWE	823	5	3 951	89 500
14	Ferranti	UK	633	16	727	20 454
15	Philips Kommunikations Ltd	GER	614	17	704	9 810
16	AEG-Telefunken	GER	565	6	3 596	73 000
17	Thomson-CSE	FRA	529	7	3 392	64 200
18	Smiths Industries	UK	498	19	497	10 864
19	Norsk Data	NOR	448	21	155	2 214
20	Lucas Industries	UK	353	12	1 788	65 485

Table 1.2 The electronics firms of the world

Rank	Company	Country	Turnover—1984 ($bn)
1	IBM	US	45.9
2	ATT	US	33.2
3	G.E.	US	27.9
4	Hitachi	Japan	21.0
5	Siemens	Germany	16.1
6	Philips	Netherlands	15.2
7	Toshiba	Japan	13.9
8	ITT	US	12.7
9	Xerox	US	8.8
10	NEC	Japan	7.6
11	Mitsubishi	Japan	7.3
12	Fujitsu	Japan	6.4
13	Hewlett–Packard	US	6.3
14	DEC	US	6.2
15	GEC	UK	6.1
16	Honeywell	US	6.1
17	TRW	US	6.1
18	Motorola	US	5.5
19	Sperry	US	5.4
20	CDC	US	5.0

Table 1.3 Telecommunications equipment, 1983

	Market (%)	Manufacture (%)
USA	41	38
Japan	7	9
Rest of world	12	11
Total ($bn)	39	42

Europe, we have 40 per cent of the world market and, in fact, we manufacture 42 per cent of the world's product. That does not sound too bad and seems rather better than the USA. At that date, 1983, Japan was quite a minor producer, but has increased its share quite dramatically since then. When you actually come to look at the details, you begin to get a bit worried.

If you actually look at what goes on in Europe, you find that we all have our 'chosen son' (Table 1.4). In the UK, you see Plessey, GEC, and STC. Due to protectionism, each country has its own industry which has fed its own internal requirements, but it has not built up to any significant extent, with the exception of Ericssons, into a world market. If you now look at our telecommunications manufacturers in Europe on a world scale, you find that sort of picture (Table 1.5).

Table 1.4 Switching equipment, European manufacturers, and market shares (%)

Firm	UK	France	W. Germany	Italy	Netherlands
Plessey	40				
GEC	40				
ITT	20	42	30	20	25
CIT-Aliatel		40			
Ericsson		18		15	
Siemens			55		
Telefunken			15		
Italtel				50	
GTE				15	
Philips					75

Just have a look at what could have happened if the Monopolies Commission had actually permitted the GEC the takeover of Plessey. That takeover bid was associated with the business of rationalizing the telecommunications field. You can see GEC in 11th place, and Plessey at 14th place. If you stick GEC and Plessey together, GEC remains at 11th place in Table 1.5.

If we look at the position for integrated circuits, only one European firm appears in the top 10 of integrated circuits manufactures, and that is Philips (Table 1.6). The top British firm probably comes in at about 27th in the world league table. That is not to say that we are not always as innovative and good in particular

Table 1.5 Telecommunications equipment sales, 1984

Position	Company	Country	$bn	As % of total sales
1	AT & T	US	10.2	31
2	ITT	US	4.7	34
3	Siemens	W. Germany	3.4	20
4	Northern Telecom	Canada	3.3	100
5	Ericsson	Sweden	3.2	90
6	IBM	US	3.0	7
7	Motorola	US	2.9	52
8	NEC	Japan	2.7	36
9	Alcatel Thomson	France	2.6	80
10	GTE	US	2.3	16
11	GEC	UK	1.4	20
12	Philips	Holland	1.2	7
13	Fujitsu	Japan	1.0	18
14	Plessey	UK	0.9	48

Table 1.6 Ranking of world integrated circuits manufacturers, 1983

Rank	Company	Home base	IC sales ($m)
1	Texas Instruments	US	1 300
2	IBM	US	1 300
3	Hitachi	Japan	1 000
4	NEC	Japan	900
5	Motorola	US	800
6	Philips	Europe	800
7	National Semiconductor	US	800
8	Fujitsu	Japan	700
9	Intel	US	700
10	Toshiba	Japan	600

ways. For example, Ferranti with their CDI process had a world-beating process for a time a couple of years ago; actually, we headed the world league table for gate arrays. That was a sheer accident; they thought they saw a niche in the market, but failed to realize just how big that niche was! All credit to them that they went for it, and they actually became the leaders in gate arrays in the world for a short

period (of course, they are being overtaken now by the big manufacturers, particularly in Japan).

Let us look at the situation regarding computers (Table 1.7).
Personally, I am very proud that ICL is a British firm and that we
have kept a major design manufacturing capability in this country,
because there are very few other countries outside the United States
and now Japan who have actually done it. You can see that Siemens
is well ahead of ICL, but that is really all on hardware, not just
computer systems. ICL are in 20th position in that table. The table is
not complete: I have just picked out the European firms below tenth
place. You can argue about the details, but the hard fact of the matter
is that we in Europe are way down the table.

Table 1.7 The leading computer firms, 1984 (extract from
Datamation 100)

Rank	Company	DP revenue ($m)
1	IBM	44 300
2	DEC	6 230
3	Burroughs	4 500
4	CDC	3 760
5	NCR	3 670
6	Fujitsu	3 500
7	Sperry	3 470
8	Hewlett–Packard	3 400
9	NEC	2 800
10	Siemens	2 790
13	Olivetti	2 012
16	Bull	1 560
20	ICL	1 220
21	Nixdorf	1 150
22	L. M. Ericsson	1 123
26	Philips	1 090

Software is an interesting field to look at because I and my
European colleagues all believe that the UK is rather good at
producing it. I remember once in the ESPRIT Management Committee, daring to remark that we really did have, in the UK, some
problems in the area of software and there were cries of protest from
around the table, all the other countries in Europe saying: 'Well if
you're in trouble, what about us'.

The fact of the matter is that the great British independent software industry comes in only three places in the top twenty and even there Logica just sneaks in at 20th position (Table 1.8). In fact, it is a pretty flat table, but if you watch what is going on in France, you can see them putting together their software industry in much larger units and buying into the United States, which is all really rather worrying for us.

It leads us, I think, to the inexorable conclusion that we have got to co-operate if we are going to be able to survive as a manufacturing nation to support service industry in this sort of field. That is what has happened in recent years in Europe in a very big way. The reasons are obvious enough, if you are in a situation where the manufacture is really now a small part of the cost, and so much of it is, then the obvious thing to do is to get together to share the costs and risks of research and development, and that is just what has been happening. We have seen the industries of other fields getting together into larger and larger units. Here, in a Unilever building I do not have to refer to the way in which the chemical industry came together; I suppose that was the end of the last century. Steel, chemicals, oil, aircraft (how many people will remember that there were 14 different aircraft manufacturing firms in the United Kingdom in 1946?), space, automobiles, and so on, all combined in much the same way. There are different ways of getting together; you do not necessarily have to merge, be taken over—you can do it, perhaps, through some form of co-operative effort.

I think you all expect, from what I said earlier about the way that technology is going, that we are going to have to stay very close to our science base to make a success. That means getting firms and the academic world close together. That, I think, is one of the important developments which has taken place in the UK, as elsewhere, in recent years.

If you are actually dealing with the R & D side, you have three stages of risk: first of all, when you do not really know whether you can actually make the thing work, you have the risk that it will not work but when you have actually got to that point, you have still got the economic risk; will it actually work in the market economically, can you actually do it for an economic price? I have always been very proud of the EMI brain scanner team, partly because the work was actually supported by my establishment for pattern recognition work for years, before actually finally somebody took some notice of the work and took it up.

Table 1.8 Computing services companies in Western Europe

	Company	Country of origin	No. of employees	Western European revenue (%M)	Worldwide revenue (%M)
1	IBM–INS	US	—	260.0	—
2	CAP Gemini Sogeti	France	3 700	151.8	207.7
3	CISI	France	2 680	138.7	172.7
4	SG2	France	4 300	135.6	150.7
5	GSi	France	2 500	132.0	135.9
6	Geisco	US	1 075	110.8	424.2
7	DATEV	W. Germany	1 882	109.9	109.9
8	Scicon	UK	2 880	105.9	138.3
9	SEMA	France	2 300	84.6	115.2
10	CCMC	France	1 250	82.7	83.5
11	Sligos	France	1 940	79.1	82.4
12	Telesystemes	France	1 750	72.1	73.6
13	Thorn-EMI	UK	1 854	68.1	104.9
14	Sesa	France	1 140	63.2	80.0
15	Volmac	Netherlands	1 270	62.1	62.1
16	Steria	France	1 380	56.8	58.6
17	Datema	Sweden	1 100	42.9	45.1
18	CIG	Belgium	550	45.3	60.9
19	NCR	US	620	44.2	140.0
20	Logica	UK	1 567	39.6	49.0

However, the interesting thing to me is that during the period when they were actually developing the brain scanner they got the scientific idea, they knew what they were going to do with it, but they were convinced that the Americans must be onto the idea too. However, since EMI were not even in the medical electronics field and there were giants in the American market already in the medical electronics field, they could very easily have lost every penny that they laid out in the development of the brain scanner. As it was, by one of those nice chances, they were able to come to the market before anybody else had actually stumbled on the idea and, at least for a period of time, they were able to dominate the field.

It is interesting to speculate what might have happened if they had chosen to licence round the world instead of trying to manufacture. I often think that it is ironic that the thing that actually went wrong with the brain scanner, on EMI's part, was essentially that they decided they couldn't continue not to manufacture in the States and they actually put the Mark II, or the Mark III, or whatever it was, into the States for manufacture rather than to continue to do it in this country. Just to show that it is not always this country which lets us down on these sort of stages, they were totally let down by the contractors that they had chosen to do this in the United States and the result was the competition got to the market place with the Mark II, or whatever, first. It is a real Greek tragedy actually; you can understand the decision which was made in the boardroom, you can only sympathize with the tragedy which from an industrial point of view occurred.

So then, you have got this third risk: would it be successful in the market place? Even when they had brought it to the market place, they had the risk that the medical profession for some reason or other would not choose to take it up. Now these risks are all compounded so that in fact the risk the firm takes on when it starts on the game is much bigger than the risk when it actually gets through the process. That is obvious enough, but in a sense it explains why co-operation on research and development is worth doing at the moment.

Co-operation on technology is what most of us have been doing, we call it pre-competitive research and development (although I never know what the word pre-competitive really means, I tend to say it rather fast to get past). On the whole the best definition is that pre-competitive research and development is any form of research and development where firms are prepared to co-operate. I admit that it is a bit circular, but you could carry on and you could take research and development nearer to the market place, you could get into demonstrations. The Alvey programme has a limited number of big demonstration projects in it.

I think the next wave of collaboration that we can see, is in the plans for ESPRIT 2 and the programme of the Bide Committee which is looking at what should be done after Alvey. I think the next waves are actually going to have in them much more work nearer to the market place, nearer to products if you like. Let us take it into the second stage, to demonstration say. We have learnt to co-operate, we can face up to that. In the meanwhile, along has come Eureka and, as least as far as the French and the UK are concerned, it is actually about the lot—it is about high technology, risky projects, but it is not just about co-operation on technology. It is very much about co-operation on the production and the marketing side. If you like, particularly for high technology products, it is about co-operation in marketing.

The production side of it is really becoming, unfortunately for employment, not very important. Only a few years ago, how many factories did we have in this country manufacturing telephone equipment? Half a dozen? One factory could now supply all the telephone exchange equipment required for Europe. The Alvey programme is actually supported by the Department of Trade and Industry, Ministry of Defence, and the Science and Engineering Research Council. It is also supported by industry, who fund half the cost. My directorate is a very peculiar beast in the organization of such things because although I am a civil servant, I have in my directorate people from these three departments and from industry. I have people seconded from industry working within the director-ate: the firms actually pay their salaries and we work as a common team.

Well, I won't go through the details of this, the fact is that by my standards Alvey was a large programme, £350 millions over 5 years, £200 million to the government (Table 1.9). You will notice, of course, a 50/50 shared programme between industry and the government—a £350 million programme, including £200 million from the government (that's the meaning of 50/50 in our world). You will not be surprised at the subjects which we are covering; they are very largely the subjects that I have spoken about earlier on such as VSLI, CAD for VSLI, Software Engineering, Intelligent Know-ledge Based Systems (IKBS), Man–Machine Interactions (MMI),

Table 1.9 Participation, June 1986

	Alvey	ESPRIT
Cost to UK	£200 M	£100 M
Projects	187	190
UK firms	109 (428 entries)	50 (165 entries)
UK universities	53 (237 entries)	33 (56 entries)
UK polytechnics	12 (17 entries)	5 (5 entries)
UK 'establishments'	20 (45 entries)	13 (18 entries)
Total participation	194 (727 entries)	101 (244 entries)

and Networks. We are also very much a partner in the European programme ESPRIT.

The ESPRIT programme in the United Kingdom is half the size of the Alvey programme, but of course, because it covers the twelve countries of the European Community, it is a much bigger programme overall (Table 1.9). As far as the UK is concerned, it costs about £100 million over 5 years. That is the cost to the tax payer. ESPRIT is dominated by the big twelve information technology companies of Europe. I personally do not object to this as 85 per cent or more of the market of the European manufacturers of IT lies with those twelve firms. Of course it would be a tragedy if the voice of only those twelve was heard because perhaps that would be the voice of a dinosaur. It would be very unfortunate if smaller firms did not get a look in.

If you make a comparison of these two 5-year programmes, roughly running over the same period, we are now $3\frac{1}{2}$ years or so through both programmes and virtually committed. I have already said that the ESPRIT programme in the UK is about half the size of the Alvey programme, although it has roughly the same number of projects (you would expect that in a sense because the ESPRIT programme has, of course, got European partners in it, whereas the Alvey programme has only got British partners).

The Alvey programme of about 100 firms, includes quite a number of small firms, too. The ESPRIT programme has got about 50 British firms in it and every university in the United Kingdom takes part, although not quite so many really take part. I think that is probably because we have not yet learnt to take advantage of these

European programmes in all parts of our industrial and academic society.

Then along came the European Cooperation in High Technology Projects for Industrial Prosperity (Eureka). Eureka came, to some extent, like a rabbit out of the hat—some people say that President Mitterand announced it as the attempt to carry out a European SDI. The fact of the matter is that Eureka was seen by Mitterand as a way of bringing the industry of Europe together to re-vitalize it and to use European industry as a springboard to the European markets and the world. Much to his surprise, the United Kingdom very rapidly responded and became, at least at Government level, a very keen supporter of Eureka. I am quite confident that if it had not been for the experience of working in the Alvey and the ESPRIT programmes we would not have got the sort of response we have got from industry.

France launched the programme in 1985 and began to establish it. Then the Germans took over and to everybody's surprise, and to my astonishment, the British Government volunteered to become the third Chairman of the Eureka process, no mean ordeal. I have to say that I was very much involved, but it was my colleagues who really did the work: I merely acted as orator. There are 18 nations of Eureka and you can imagine getting the 19 now involved (EEC 12, EFTA 6, and Turkey) and the EEC Commission to reach an agreement on the procedures. Even getting agreement on what it is all about was no mean feat, and I am very proud of my colleagues, who did so much, and I have to say that the French press have acknowledged the very considerable part that the UK have played in getting this lined up.

It was finally decided to follow the principles laid down in the Hanover Declaration in November 1985, and the procedures and Secretariat agreed in London in June 1986, with the brief to cover projects in all high technology fields. By June 1986, 72 projects were established, 10 in November 1985 and 62 in June 1986. UK firms are involved in 29 projects, the average cost of each project being £25 million, although some have cost over £200 million. The costs are broken down as follows:

(1) Information Technology—42 per cent;
(2) Advanced Manufacturing—18 per cent;
(3) New Materials—12 per cent;
(4) Biotechnology—12 per cent;

(5)   Environmental and Transport—12 per cent;
(6)   Marine Technology—1 per cent.

Market opening measures are to be targeted through the projects.

Rather strangely, we and the French find ourselves as natural allies in this and are working well together on Eureka. Remember the projects involved are much bigger, on average, than the sort of projects I was talking about in ESPRIT and Alvey. There are some quite small ones because, of course, they are directed at the market place and they have got co-operation right the way through.

I think I ought to finish on a cautious note. Although I have spoken very largely about co-operation as being the way forward, I am not, in any way, saying that mergers, take-overs, and so on are not also necessary. What I have not yet clearly said is that I do believe that there is a role in the United Kingdom for the entrepreneurial firm in all this.

In the Alvey programme, there are a considerable number of these firms and I think all of us involved with them, get enormous satisfaction out of them. I do not know how many of you have actually been involved in the Cambridge phenomenon, but I can assure you I think that it is perhaps one of the greatest pleasures of my working life to have been involved in that. To go into a firm like Acorn, despite its history, of an evening, has been a most exciting experience. You find there a crowd of people, busily working late into the night; of course, you cannot tell whether they are actually full-time employers of Acorn, Dons in the University, postgraduate students, or undergraduates.

There is an interesting tradition in Cambridge, which has built up around the high-tech firms, when Acorn was struggling to get the BBC micro out on time. Of course, they were late in the inevitable way of these sort of things, the teams were working late at night, and it got to the point where the Managing Director realized that he could not allow this to go on. So he used to come round at about 9 o'clock and sweep them all up and say, enough is enough, come and have dinner. It became known in the University that if you wanted to contact these people, you had to go to a particular pub after 9 o'clock. The result was, that some of the dons who were intimately interested in what was going on, used to go there and got some of their best ideas in that pub; this has spread to other firms in the Cambridge phenomenon.

Acorn has had its difficulties. I personally think that the story is not all a tragedy. Olivetti are actually handling them, in my view more sensibly. They now have, if you like, a Dutch uncle (I prefer not to say a big brother): somebody who can protect them, can help them through, and I personally believe we will see them having a good, strong future. It is very difficult for somebody of my generation to feel that the fact that it is now owned by a foreign firm is something that is very wrong. If you were in one part of the United States and it was a firm in another part of the United States who owned the small entrepreneurial firm you might not think there was anything wrong or strange about that.

I do think we have our real difficulties in coping with these entrepreneurial firms. You have only to look at the field of integrated circuits, for example, to see the way it is new firms which have come through and created the market there. Of the top 10, there is only one firm in the top 10 now making integrated circuits who made electronic valves. Perhaps that is some indication of dinosaurs. On the whole in Europe, and it is as true of Germany as it is of the UK, we have been singularly unsuccessful in bringing these small firms through to success.

There are outstanding examples, we all know them. My favourite is Oxford Instruments. I have to say that, because having praised the Cambridge phenomenon I have to remember my roots, and in fact Oxford Instruments started out at the physics laboratories in Oxford. It was nursed on numerous occasions by my department, and ran very close to the financial edge on more than one occasion.

Finally their day came: You probably know the great success story. Their superconducting magnets are the leaders in the world and they go from strength to strength. Well, that one I think has actually made it into the big time. Logica made it into the big time; they had a bad year last year, but once again they've recovered this year, and I would like to think that a considerable number of the Cambridge phenomenon will make it. Here, in the Kingston area, we have quite a thriving undercurrent of these small firms.

I suspect that we have got to learn a good deal more about this game, perhaps in our academic days, than we do at the moment, and I personally think that one of the big benefits that is going to come from this new wave of co-operation between the academic and industrial world is that the academic teaching will itself subtly change. Only a few years ago, it really wasn't very respectable to be seen as a director of a company if you were in the senior common room. Now, of course, it is perfectly respectable to be working closely with firms.

I think the way in which the students develop their attitude to industry and to success (profit if you like), will be subtly changed. We may find that we can breed a set of entrepreneurs. We will have no difficulty on the technology side. I do not have to go into the evidence for that, as it is absolutely clear that if what we are looking for is the people with ideas and the ability to initiate them, we have it. We have it as much in technology as we have it in science. Our difficulty is to turn that into economic success, and maybe if there is a different outlook to profit and so on, we will find ourselves with a whole new raft of successful high technology industry.

Frankly, I sincerely hope so because I have to say if this country is not going to succeed in high technology industries then I think the future is extremely bleak for us.

2 Implications for education and training

CHRIS HUMPHRIES

I do not wish to consider current AIT applications, things happening now. Those who work in Kingston College of Further Education are very aware of new technology because its IT Development Unit is a superb facility for research and development within both the further education curriculum and the field of company-led training. For those of you who are not in Kingston there is plenty of general discussion about the implications of AIT still available. What I wish to do is to try and look ahead, a little way in terms of technology, but actually a long way in terms of our understanding of how people learn, so as to explore the real role new technology can play in advancing the nature of education and training in the United Kingdom.

To begin, let me postulate: 'AIT makes it much easier for education and training to do all the things they always wanted to do'. Just about everyone has either said or agreed this over the past 3 years. It has been said about every technological input into education and training since Gutenberg. Now, contrast this theory with the one I would offer; namely, 'AIT makes it much easier for education and training to do all the things they *never* wanted to do'. I suggest the second one touches upon a crucial problem of AIT applications. Properly used they can open up genuine avenues for progress, but they also provide an opportunity to worsen all the learning practices and training methods that are already ineffective. Though this is a broad summary, it points none the less to an essential difficulty we have to face when considering the value of AIT in education and training.

AIT has a number of features of its own which may be itemized as follows:

(1) advanced hardware;
(2) advanced software;
(3) advanced programming techniques.

Brian Oakley has indicated some of the directions these developments are likely to take and the possibilities they may offer in a broad sense. Since my focus is learning, it seems to me that AIT specifically offers:

(1)   new education and training tools;
(2)   adaptive learning systems;
(3)   improved understanding of learning and learning processes.

By the concept of a tool, I mean anything that supports the success or effectiveness involved in an educational or a training exercise. Whether it be a skills training exercise aimed at improving the abilities of people working on a production line or adapting their mode of operation to newly introduced technology, or whether it be a highly intellectual activity involving deep cognitive processes, a tool remains something that assists learning achievement, with or without a computer.

The tool is what the learner or trainee sees. It might be a book or a video. The latter could be watched right through or in parts following the completion of set tasks. Both of these tools represent, one might say, the obvious or apparent structure of the learning experience that has been created. This is the top level.

A second level, however, relates to what I term the learner–machine interface and concerns the message which is being imparted. What understanding are we trying to create? Is it something as basic as how to operate a control panel or is it something as deep as an appreciation of new management techniques?

The third level of learning is found in the organization of the material used. What exercises or techniques, are the learners expected to go through? Are they expected to sit in a room and listen to a lecture? Or are they expected to sit in front of a piece of technology and work through that? Is the learning taking place in the workplace, in a college, at home, or even at sea? (Fig. 2.1).

Another consideration must be whether the learning takes place in a class, a small group, or individually. What we are addressing here are methods of learning. The last level, as shown in Fig. 2, consists of the assumptions made about the processes of learning. How do people best learn this particular type of skill or come to understand the meaning of this particular piece of information? What methods or approaches should we adopt in order to instruct someone efficiently and effectively in the operation of a numerically

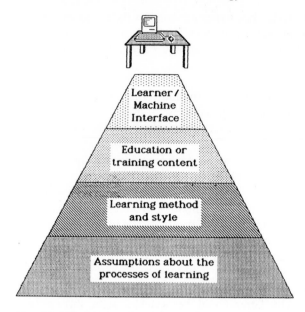

Fig. 2.1 Education and training tools.

controlled machine-tool? What sort of learning experience is best offered to a management trainee studying time management?

The sheer variety of motives for learning is enormous. One learner is sent by a company, another chooses to enhance qualifications, a third has a personal interest, a fourth has a private project in mind. Although their reasons for study may be very different, each person has one thing in common, a desire for a learning process that is as easy and as effective as possible. It is an assumption on the part of the learner that we have to take into full account. Indeed, it is the only basis upon which we can reasonably apply new technology.

How then does AIT interact with the various levels of learning I have outlined? What contribution can we hope AIT to make to any of them? Perhaps we ought to admit that, at the moment, the answer is very little. Take, for instance, numerically controlled machine-tools. The decision about a course is going to be based on an assessment of the learner's work needs and the company's employment needs. Neither the learner nor the employer are likely to have given much thought to learning assumptions. These are left to the course organizers, whether a further education college, a commercial training company, or an equipment manufacturer. In this context AIT becomes important, however, for it offers possibilities that no previous advances in technology have offered. It does make things so much easier for learning, but it also makes undesirable things so much easier too.

Fundamental to this problem is the drastic change taking place today in the structure of education and training. The days are long past when learning occurred in institutions with clearly defined priorities. Open Learning and Open Tech has brought about a significant upsurge of company-based training. No longer are technical colleges the only major providers for the post-compulsory sector of education. The recently announced Open College will obviously need to collaborate with colleges of further education, yet there will be nothing to be gained by any decision to restrict its activities to the present education system. One of its vital links is bound to be with the 150 industry-based projects run under the Open Tech scheme sponsored by the Manpower Services Commission. Then again, there are the proposed City Technical Colleges to be considered, apart from commercial training companies. We might even see Open School yet. The current attempt to increase school contacts with industry and the community at large is a step in this direction. All I am saying is that any assumptions we may hold about monopoly providers have to be discarded, because it is a fact that we are living in an increasingly flexible education and training world.

This explains, in part, the amazing upsurge in the development of in what is termed 'stand alone' learning packages. This learning method is an interesting model for us to examine, not least because its failure can often be traced to an obvious oversight; namely, that most learning takes place between human beings. Nevertheless, 'stand alone' learning packages are becoming big business as they move into the field of interactive video, which is seen to have great potential in industrial training.

Consider then this model as that of the learning experience, and at the same time examine the input AIT may have to its effectiveness. It can be shown diagrammatically (Fig. 2.2). It is certainly a simple model, but this is how the design of many learning packages operate. As yet, commercial training companies have hardly begun to focus on the learning processes themselves. They tend to assume that the content of their packages should receive the bulk of attention, leaving the isolated learner in Fig. 2.2 to cope as best he can. A genuine appreciation of what makes for effective learning is often

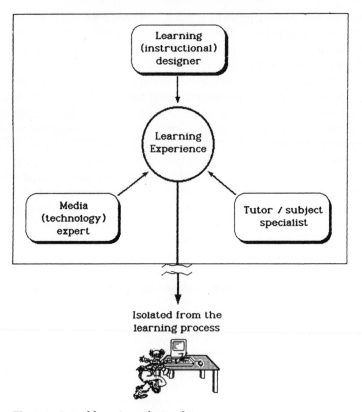

Fig. 2.2 Actual learning relationships.

lacking, for the reason that the perceived processes involved are shown in Fig. 2.3.

Change is coming, but I am afraid only at a very slow pace. Light may be shed on some of the problems by the work now being done at Southampton University, where an attempt is in progress to create an interactive video package with what is loosely described as having a degree of 'intelligence'. What researchers there hope to create is a package with four different learning styles or approaches, based on four different theories about how learning takes place. When complete, the package will be used to investigate how the materials in it can be made more effective, by comparison between the results derived from each style. The content issue is not as central as some people believe.

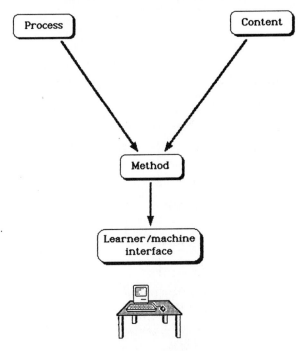

Fig. 2.3 Perceived learning relationships.

Figure 2.4 shows a schematic view of the relations involved in the learning process. The design of a learning experience has to be sensitive to all of them. The learner–machine interface (rather than man/woman–machine interface) must be attractive: a well produced book, video, or CBT package. This is significant because of how the material is presented affects the possibilities of learning, especially at a distance. It inevitably represents both the learning style and the assumptions behind the package.

However, the difficulty here is that actual learning relations are much more complicated than the diagram can possibly indicate. Helping people to learn is an immensely complex task, a fact that we are gradually coming to realize. Theories outnumber answers; all I can say is I do not know how people learn.

The same realization is becoming general among the AIT people who are working on learning materials. The interaction between the learning package and human learning process is hard to grasp (Fig. 2.5). Yet it is obvious that value in learning can be expected

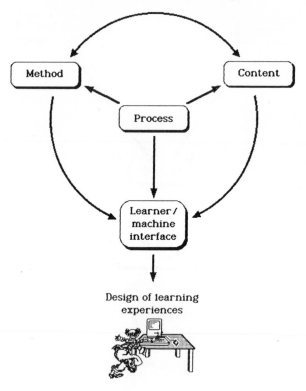

Fig. 2.4 Designing learning tools.

where the interaction is two-way. In learning there is always more than content, as any teacher knows. There is the learning about how to learn and adapt to future learning, which goes on all the time. Adapting and updating of existing knowledge can never be simply the passing across of further information, if only because the way in which a learning experience occurs produces a mental set about the learning itself. There is literally no way that teaching can happen without teaching both method and content.

It follows therefore that our understanding of a learning process which necessarily embraces content and method has a profound effect on how we present and structure the learning material. The overall process is, in effect, a line of learning experiences, which properly combined together can form valuable learning opportunities, packages, or courses.

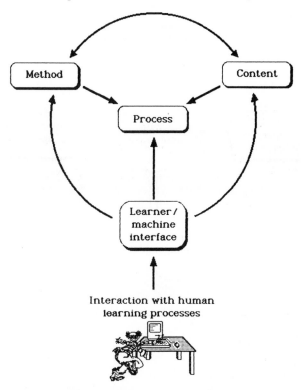

Fig. 2.5 Added value to learning.

Where does AIT fit into all this? The short answer is that it facilitates the design of packages by allowing adaptive learning (Fig. 2.6). Thus, the two-way flow of information (as shown in the arrows) allows validation, evaluation, and assessment, not of the student, but of the effectiveness of the learning package. It monitors the package design and, in turn, adds to our knowledge of the learning process. Although it is still early days, an efficient adaptive learning system should:

(1) accept and respond to a wide variety of learning styles:
(2) adapt to the responses of the learner;
(3) adapt to the user's learning style;
(4) allow full learner 'tailoring';
(5) allow learner to override at 'all' times;

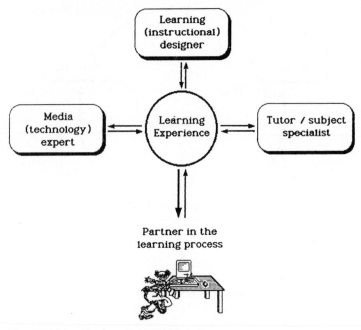

Fig. 2.6 Adaptive learning systems.

(6)   record data on user's style for future use;
(7)   'record' details relevant to the learning process for designers;
(8)   record learning management information.

This means the expertise of many specialists will have to be pooled to achieve such a system: learning methods, new technology, programming, graphic design, and video are all needed.

The gap is, of course, the learner. Where is the positive feed-back from the student? This is the nub of the matter. The traditional gap between the design of learning materials and the learner has to be broken down. Unless we arrange things in such a way that the learner has some say in what he is learning and where it is learned, then learning opportunities will not be enhanced by the adoption of AIT. Without interaction or feed-back during learning, there can be no possibility of an individual approach. Since AIT ought to be capable of an individual approach, in the not too distant future, it seems absurd not to put our efforts into developing adaptive learning systems. 'Interactive learning systems' is now a popular buzz phrase. This is a pity because, as presently conceived, an interactive system allows individual control within fairly strict limits. The parameters are narrow in comparison with the adaptive learning model I believe we should be aiming for.

AIT (in preference to terms like Artificial Intelligence and Expert Systems) gives us the opportunity of trying to build adaptive learning systems that can work with and understand the way in which the learner wants to think, the way in which a learner wants to utilize knowledge, and so, in the process, restructure the way that information is presented. STC Technology Limited is already building an 'Interactive Dialogue System' for BT Gold, the electronic mail system. What they are attempting to do, in conjunction with British Telecom and several universities, is to create a means of access for all potential users of BT Gold. The idea is that as soon as a would-be user communicates through the keyboard, it begins to judge the degree of experience the user possesses, so as to offer the most suitable way into what is a very complex mail system. If it discovers, for instance, that typing is a problem, it will offer a menu system instead. If long pauses happen, it will assume hurried reference to the instruction manual and indicate what should be done next. Though still at an early stage, and in human terms an exceedingly primitive approach, the point to note is that the designers are addressing the uncertainties of the user; they are identifying areas of ignorance and at a simple level making a computer 'people literate'.

Because technology is not usually sensitive to the problems encountered by people when they try to use it, this reversal is noteworthy. Let us remember that it is feasible for computers to store information about human foibles and to respond to recognized difficulties in a supportive manner. Hence, adaptive systems would commence interaction with a general assessment of what the user expects to gain, then store this information and any details of how the user prefers to work, before deciding on the best approach to offer. Another application could be as a monitoring device within an existing computer system. One MSC project is concerned with the analysis of mistakes made within the insurance industry, by means of an embedded system, in order to build up a realistic picture of training needs.

It is evident that 'adaptive' technology does not imply a tremendous advance so much as a rethinking of present possibilities. The method is Expert Systems, the object is easier access, easier use.

Concentration on user friendliness is central to the earlier question of overcoming the isolation of the learner, stuck before the screen. As a result of the attention given to the user-machine interface over the past 3 years, we have seen a coming together of technical improvements and instructional design, a symbiosis that has led to the 'Interactive Dialogue System' already described. The overflow into educational software has also happily left behind the dispiriting 'No—you are wrong'. Instead, the Expert System now explains the reasons for the incorrect answer, or it can do so, providing it has been included in the software design.

Research in schools has revealed that some pupils can become more interested in the noise computers make when an answer is incorrect than in finding out the reasons for error. Software engineers who overlook 'technological naughtiness' have failed to take account of the motivation of the user. However, AIT should reverse this situation, since psychologists and technologists are combining to tailor packages much more to user needs. Hesitancy and uncertainty on the learner's part are now being incorporated in the design of learning styles, with menus offering alternative approaches when required. There can be no question in the foreseeable future of AIT causing the replacement of the book (which remains a very convenient piece of technology), but none the less the instructional and learning edge that adaptive learning packages clearly offer cannot be discounted. At certain levels and for certain purposes, they provide excellent tools for education and training.

Flicking through a book is easy to do; so far this is proving a difficult task on a screen. Such 'tailoring' will become commonplace in videos over time, as the facility is already available via a special computer program from a few video disks. When this level of flexibility is general though, the opportunities for individual learning, especially at a distance, will be tremendously enhanced. The ability to use AIT with this ease will be what 'computer literacy' means in future. It will, of course, make people less dependent on the technology of the book, thereby signalling the end of four centuries of Gutenburg's total influence on the dissemination of knowledge. This will be particularly true as machines develop 'people literacy' and learn to adapt to individual learning requirements. Then it will dawn on us how inert, how structurally static, the printed page really is.

What all this leaves us is with an urgent need to admit the complexity of the learning process. We have to acknowledge where teaching and training practice is wrong. We must identify the strengths and weaknesses of different learning strategies. Throwing learning packages at students, individually or in groups, will achieve nothing without a prior coming together of educational psychologists and technological researchers.

The insight offered on learning in *Understanding Schools as Organisations* is instructive. Charles Handy and Robert Aitken (1986) have recently demonstrated the oddness of the teacher's role in that judgement is not made on how learning is managed, but on how much the pupils have learned. With AIT opening up possibilities of more individual modes of learning, it is clear that the perceived responsibilities of the teacher will have to change. Part of certification may have to be organized automatically through the computer-based learning system. The implications of greater learner responsibility are of course profound. The balance of expectation is bound to shift, freeing both teacher and pupil from many of the custodial assumptions that have crippled schools.

At the moment, I believe that we all have a strong image of education. It figures a group in a classroom, sitting down before a teacher, with a book or a video, and learning something. The mediator is the teacher. No scope is available in this situation for individual enquiry on the lines of the TAPS project under MSC sponsorship. The Training Access Points System is aimed at the needs of small businesses, and it is the first phase of an attempt to create a national electronic data system of information on all the learning and training opportunities in the United Kingdom. The second phase of the project is concerned with putting at the front of the data base an Expert System capable of analysing the training needs of the enquirer prior to providing appropriate information about where they can be met.

A common problem of small businesses is control of cash-flow, but closer investigation reveals that problems here arise from a number of different sources. Where TAPS will help and have a dynamic function is in the collection of data about this range of difficulty. In effect, it will be a technological training needs analyst. While individual businessmen will receive help with their special problems, TAPS will collect and analyse the general nature of the overall pattern too. It will help to educate trainers about training needs. A similar system to TAPS is dealing with adult careers guidance.

Industrial problem-solving is also susceptible to Expert Systems. The Industry and Commerce Group at Kingston is already offering such a service, as is the Open University. What is showing up is that many problems stem from personal relationships, from an insufficient grasp on how human beings interact. Computer modelling of human interaction does not mean the replacement of human beings, but rather a means to better understanding of inter-personal relationships. Both managers and staff can learn from such knowledge.

Expert Systems are knowledge bases coerced from human experts. Just now, exactly what they are providing educators and trainers is unclear. Easier to grasp are the advantages offered in, for example, medical diagnosis, where symptoms fall readily into categories. Other kinds of expertise does not lend itself so conveniently to elicitation. Because Expert Systems are rule-based systems, they are most suited to knowledge which can be rigorously defined and structured, like the symptoms associated with specific diseases and conditions. Yet again, the development of Expert Systems is incidentally helping us to understand how knowledge is organized by the mind. Current research in the field of knowledge representation in computers cannot fail to enlarge the awareness of educators and trainers.

Let me end with some predictions, though I had better admit that I am uncertain as to whether they would occur by the year 2000. Here are a few directions I believe research and development will have to take:

(1)   user/machine interface;
(2)   education through 'advisor' systems;
(3)   modelling of human interactions;
(4)   management of learning;
(5)   processes of knowledge elicitation;
(6)   transfer of non-technology learning.

The last one brings me back to my original comment: we need to be as concerned to improve the quality of education and training outside the realm of new technology as we need to improve their quality within it. The one advantage new technology offers us is insight into the learning process, which we disregard at our peril.

At Vancouver, in 1986, the biggest conference ever held on education took place. Almost 10 000 delegates attended 450 sessions, spread over 1 week and, needless to say, a key issue was new technology. The general view there was that the United Kingdom is still out in front in terms of educational technology. What impressed delegates was the commonsense approach of our teachers and trainers, and their genuine interest in experimenting with computers in the learning situation. Because of this sensible flexibility, Britain should be very well placed to handle the massive future changes to be wrought by AIT. Where we score again and again is in the excellence of an institution like Kingston College of Further Education, which has pioneered the application of Expert Systems to practical problems in education and training. The IT Development Unit is a model for coping with technological change because its philosophy is a realistic involvement of both staff and students in exploring the learning implications of AIT. Though this may seem commonsense, the experience of the USA, Canada, and Japan shows how disastrous it is when this does not occur. Since in Britain there is an appreciation of the need for co-operation between those who develop new technological applications and those who use them in learning, I am personally hopeful that AIT will have a beneficial effect. An effect, however, it certainly will have: all we can do together is to try and harness the opportunities new technology is already beginning to throw up.

3 The experience of corporate users

Experience of Information Technology at Unilever

SIR GEOFFREY ALLEN

Our subject is Information Technology in a major corporation. I will therefore talk a little bit about what goes on in Unilever and, because I am Research and Engineering Director, I will talk specifically about technological information. Unilever has a turnover of about £16 billion distributed in Europe, North America, and in the rest of the world. The heartland is Europe, but we do have substantial businesses of £3 billion in North America and some £4 billion in the other overseas countries. When you look at the shape of Unilever, you see that that £16 billion covers a multitude of sins. We have almost a third of a million people employed around the world, we are organized in 523 companies organized in seven main business areas and we work in 75 countries.

To take another view, the main business areas are edible fats, frozen food, other foods and drinks, detergents, personal products, speciality chemicals, and agribusiness (largely animal feeds at the moment).

You will recognize the names of some of our companies in the UK: Van den Berghs and Jurgens, Birds Eye Walls, Batchelors Foods, Brook Bond Oxo, John West, Lipton Export, Matteson Walls, Lever Brothers, PPF International, Crosfields, Vinamul, Elida Gibbs, Thames Board, Oxoid-Unipath, BOCM Silcock, and Marine Harvest. That will give you an idea of the size of the company and its diversity, and some of the names by which you will recognize us in the UK. It is also interesting, as an aside, to note that you will rarely find the name Unilever advertized, certainly not for any of our products.

You can imagine that with that kind of breadth, we badly need a formal information service to keep body and soul together and so,

25 years ago, it was decided that we should do something about organizing the flow of technical information in Unilever. Hans Roscoff was given the job of setting up an information system for our technologists, with the aim of getting to each technologist across the world the latest in Unilever technical information. Some of this information is generated in the Research and Engineering Laboratories (there are three, two in the UK and one in Holland), but it is also generated in factories in sixty different countries. Forty countries have development laboratories and then each business area has its co-ordination staff in the centre, which runs the particular business world-wide and of course there is also the nerve centre for collecting information.

So all the technical information floating around in this mass has to be brought together and systematized. What the early teams had to wrestle with was reports floating to and fro, and numerous manuals. In fact, I think things probably got out of hand with the variety of activities and then follow-up telephone calls, telexes, and visits. So it was really quite an exercise to reduce all this vast confused mass into some organized data bank. It was done in a way that actually has proved to be the nub of the way we are going to introduce modern Information Technology. Hans called this activity a 'technical information service', and in his 20 years, it grew from two or three people to over 60 people all in Head Office in London, organizing this flow of data.

At some stage, in those 20 years, probably about 10 years ago, they hit on what was a crucial way of focusing the flow of technology. What they did was to take about 10 very bright young technologists that had come into the centre. They made them shadow the senior technical member of each business area, so that each senior technical manager had a shadow who saw all his mail, saw all the reports he was reading or generating, and who could then begin to assess what were the key items of information that needed to be stored in the centre, for later distribution by an information service. Each of these shadows had secretaries working for them, pounding the thing out, constructing reports and goodness knows what, and making sure they were circulated to those 500 companies.

When it came to future products, and the research and development programmes, there had emerged another band called research managers. Each of the business areas had a research manager, who organized the research programme in the research laboratories. Only he actually knew all about the programmes going on in the research laboratories. He could oversee the new products being evolved and going out into the development units in the operating companies.

So we needed yet another group of shadows, another 10 bright young men who shadowed all these research managers in each of the business areas. So, we now had one set of shadows collecting the technology, and another set collecting the product information and the new ideas coming out of research. That really is the structure of the operation we have got today. In each business area, these two key people, one co-ordinating the technology in the factories, the other looking at the upgrading of existing products and the introduction of new products. Between them they control much of the information that has to be disseminated in a particular business area.

Then, of course, one has had to have some kind of communication system. This was very much by mail in the early days, but with increasing use of telephones and telexes around the world, to provide access to companies that sent in requests for Unilever knowledge. These requests are channelled through particular business areas, regardless of the country the caller is in.

The Technical Information Service undertakes the following activities:

(1) gathering, analysing, and storing technical data on manufacturing operations, products, and research and development programmes;
(2) supporting technical communications systems;
(3) providing companies with access to Unilever's knowledge;
(4) applying new Information Technology.

If, for example, you are in detergents, then your request will come up through the detergents segment of the Technical Information Service into the centre. If the people in the service can deal with it straight away, they do. If not, they will consult either the senior technical manager or one of his assistants as to what they should do about the request for information.

When you look at the new technology we are now introducing in the shape of a more sophisticated computer network, you can still see that original format of the technical service that has served us very well in the past. So I regard this part, the introduction of shadows in the centre, monitoring the key technical people in the business areas, as the absolute crux of our evolving technical service, and it will remain so. I cannot see that being dispensed with, no matter how intelligent the machines become.

More recently, in the past 5 years, the role of this group of people has been to apply new Information Technology to itself. That is, they have developed their computers and all the various programs that go with them, but before we actually look at some of the things they have done, it is worth reflecting that we had 60 people in this activity 5 years ago. We are now down to 50, although we do not think we will drop much lower than that. The volume of work, however, has gone up enormously and we have actually added two new major business areas in that time. The people numbers have come down a bit, but there was not a dramatic reduction. Rather, there has been a significant improvement in cost effectiveness.

In one sense, we would not be too keen to replace the concept of the 'shadowers'. If someone is working in one of our operating companies and he is a bright young technologist one of the best things you can do for him is send him into this Technical Information Service for a year or two. He will get a view of Unilever technology and experience that you cannot get from any other vantage point. So, for some of our top young people, this is a major career step. If you come into our technical service, you will find that half the people there are from overseas countries, including the United States, all of whom who have come in as an important part of their career development. We like having them because they are some of the best people we have got. Their companies like to send them, because of what they bring back in terms of information, and knowing not just where to go for the information, but who to talk to. They also learn to appreciate the potential benefits of computers in information such as:

(1) manipulation of data;
(2) searching of (vast amounts of) data;
(3) continuous updating;
(4) interactive systems;
(5) remote and distributed input of data;
(6) remote and distributed access.

All in all, we find it a very valuable development indeed for the running of our companies.

That is the service as it has basically become. We have now come to the question of applying new technology. What we are doing there, of course, is fairly straight forward. We use conventional machines and we buy as much software off the shelves as we can. That is only limited by this regrettable tendency that people have to write their own software and, of course, the man running TIS has to be ever watchful that his people are not writing software that he can more readily buy. For us, computers are very important, although we still have some of the old stacks of data around. We have enormous files full of letters and distillations of reports and goodness knows what. We have still got great big process manuals all stacked up in cupboards. But gradually, if you look across the offices of the TIS you will see new ways of storing vast amounts of data. They are much better not only at physical storage, but because searching and manipulation is much easier, new forms of cross-referencing of knowledge can take place, and of course, one can do continuous updating on a much more effective basis. Finally, the information can be personally retrievable by people 3000 miles away—even when they may not even be sure exactly what questions they should be asking!

Always it comes back to these bright young shadows that are watching and drawing from what the technical members are doing in co-ordination in their business area. They are there to make sure that we do not get garbage going in and, if possible, coded in such a way that very little garbage goes out.

The great thing about the computer network is that it gives us these extra powers of interaction; people can interact with the system from a distance, they can begin to ask questions of the data banks, and can reply without having to come back through the shadow or having it referred back to the technical people in their coordination.

There is nothing more destructive either of your business or of the people running it, of course, than to get ridiculous answers. One day, we will have a bigger involvement in distributed access; at the moment the access to input information is still very centralized; we still have these policemen sifting data and I think they will always be there. Maybe later, we will have distributed shadows around the world who have certain powers of input as well. We have still to get to that point, however.

The state of play in our system is perhaps best described by saying that we have some interactive computer data bases in most of our business areas. People can now get abstracts of internal reports and documents; they can search them by key words and so on, and search the databases. One can search them by problem categories or seek relationships between apparently unrelated experiences. One can get access if one is in trade with companies in Australia, or in India, or the USA. We are beginning to get international interactive intelligent systems growing up.

This takes time, and most of all it takes care. When you walk around the office now what you find is that increasingly, the secretaries who were typing out reports for the shadows have increasingly become data loggers rather than copy typists. They are the people who can take the writings, or sometimes just the key words of these bright young men, and input them directly into data banks. They have to be alert enough and clever enough to do that translation. That requires a new training and a new quality of support staff.

We rely a great deal on the 'secretaries' who have grown so much in stature. They are the crux of the chain, between the generation of the information, its sifting by the shadows and its inputting into the data banks. They too have become crucial and so again, you can see that there will still be a number of this new breed of people around. We will never, I think, get rid of the 'secretary' role, except that they will be the professional data logger with some ancillary activities on the side.

That is where we are at the moment. We have now got for our seven main business areas, this system which originally was working on the reams of paper onto the computers. Gradually, the vast amounts of paper are being replaced by computer systems advising on formulation usage and cost of raw materials, safety clearance, and usage in other countries. If you ask me what the problems are at the moment, then firstly, we have some problems in hardware. We would like nicer VDU's with more effective international communications and so on.

Secondly, we would dearly like more intelligent software so that the machine can do a lot more of the thinking, but, of course, as a technologist I do not particularly want to surrender all that to the machine. I would still like to keep a role for the bright young men who will come into the centre and do this work, and who will go out again. We still need a skeletal framework of experience, just enough experience to keep body and soul together. A lot of young men, to keep sifting, remaining alert. However, we would like a more intelligent software facility.

Thirdly, the other thing that we are still not happy with is our experience with 'electronic mail'. Electronic mail, if you read the brochure, looks fine. When you use it, it does have quite a few shortcomings. Recently, I went off to Japan, partly to see what they were doing with electronic mail. I could not find any Japanese company that was using it to any great extent! They were happy to sell it into the West, into the States, but one could not find even the people that purveyed it, using it! It is quite an issue for us. I find that people, including our customers, are rather slow to use it. When suddenly it does click, and it provides answers in 2 minutes, it turns out to be a bit too fast for people. In the end people get a bit disenchanted. Mistakes convey all too rapidly down the system and decisions are made before corrections can be applied.

So there is quite a problem here, striking the right balance and we have not got it yet. The other thing that of course we notice in TIS is the time that it takes the consumer—our field operators—to get accustomed to using the information properly. You can see in our system that there is still quite a long relaxation time, of people realizing that the material is actually available for them to get at directly. They still tend to come through the centre and, of course, quite a lot of friendships have built up this way and a few trips around the world have been generated! I hope that this will find its own level in the end, and there will be some accommodation between the need for human contact and the electronic alternative.

In my position, one has to adopt a supporting attitude to a big system like this, which is operating in a large number of companies spread around the world. I have no doubt about the way the system has improved tremendously in the last 5 years, proving very effective to distribute technology. I just get a bit frustrated when the packages fail to live up to expectations, and our users too readily fall back to the established patterns of behaviour.

Beyond the Technical Information Service, and within our three research laboratories, there are one or two experiments going on that I would just like to mention which will ultimately enhance the usefulness of the Technical Information Service. We have developed Expert Systems. In fact, much to our surprise, Alvey found that although many expert systems were mundane when they started, some of ours were amongst the few that worked. So we set up Expert Systems to try and pass on the skills of expert operators to less expert people around the world. One of the areas we chose, and I have chosen it here because it concerns Lever Brothers, was the use of spray drying towers to blow fabric washing powders. These are very complicated devices, that use a lot of energy, are very difficult to operate, blow off a lot of steam, and, of course, they handle a large number of ingredients that go into a washing powder particle.

I do not think many people realize what high technology there is in a grain of Persil. The plain fact is, an awful lot of ingredients go into a washing powder. Persil has got a surfactant to remove the dirt and impede redeposition. It needs to have a builder, usually a phosphate, that removes the hardness in the water, holds the soil in solution, and so on. You need bleach to remove the stains, and then you need an enzyme to remove some of the biological stains and assist detergency. Then you need some silica or silicate so that you do not corrode the washing machine, and then finally, a fluorescer to make things look whiter than white.

So you have all these things to go into the formulation, which must all balance with each other. You often find one or two of them will be in short supply or expensive, and you would like to put in another ingredient. What you want is an Expert System:

(1) that will tell you how to amend the formulation to get a cost effective one;
(2) that will tell you how to run your spray drying tower efficiently to get the powder you want with the chosen characteristics (summarized in Table 3.1).

Table 3.1 Knowledge systems for processing of detergent on spray-drying tower

Input data	
Given parameters	tower, e.g. inlet temperature; gas velocity
	formulation, e.g. slurry moisture content
Target parameters	processing, e.g. tower loading.
	powder, e.g. moisture; bulk density; compressibility
Output	
Estimates of	processing paramaters
	powder properties
Comments on estimates *v*. targets, e.g. satisfactory; storage problems	

Port Sunlight Laboratory have developed quite a good Expert System for this. When it was first started I had just come to Unilever, and I saw this system growing like Topsy. One day, I went to Leicester Polytechnic, where I found a young man who had got a teaching system that did rather the same thing for students except that they did not have a spray drying tower! They had an experiment in the lab and what we found was that the key to this man's success was to have a modular system, where you could call up modules that did specific jobs in terms of the total operation.

So Port Sunlight developed its own Expert System around which there was a module that dealt with formulations, one that dealt with the technology of operating the spray drying tower, another one that told you how well you were using your capital, and so on (Fig. 3.1); so that you could work out the economics of the whole operation. Then in carrying out the pilot plant trials, an operator might have half a dozen attempts at blowing a new powder, and each attempt is rather costly. So if you can train him to get there in one or two shots, that saves you a lot of money.

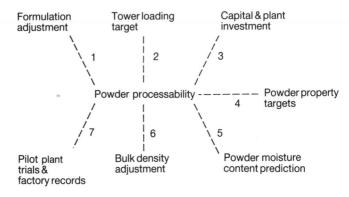

Fig. 3.1 Expert systems for the technology of operating a spray-drying tower.

Practical recommendations on the running of the tower are half technological and half folk lore. You have to know whether to kick the left leg of the spray dry tower on Monday morning before you start and which direction the wind is blowing, and things like that. So in creating this Expert System, not only was there an interest from computer staff in the organization of the software but also in the problem of getting in all the technology that we have alongside the detailed calculations that could be done by the computer. There was this other ingredient of getting in the folk lore. So we sought to interview two of our best spray drying tower operators around the world. They would tell us how to do it and that would go into the system. Simple? Well, in fact that was the most difficult bit. It is never the computer that causes the difficulty in any problem, it is the people. These experts were trying to tell us, but, of course, it had become such a habit that even they did not recognize some of the key moves they were making. By inviting one of them up to Hoylake, letting him play golf, and taking the tape recorder round as we went, we finally extracted quite a lot of this 'soft' information. That then had to be sifted, and matched with the 'hard' data, to end up with an Expert System that had folk lore, economics, and technology all intertwined.

Such a system can be made available through TIS or in the form of a stand alone Personal Computer. The kind of thing that happens is you can put in the data, what parameters you would like to have the for the inlet temperatures on the slurry, moisture content, and so on, the formulation. You can say what the target parameters are: how much you would like to blow in how many hours; the power loading; what kind of powder you want at the end (whether you want a dense powder or a light powder), and so on. The Expert System will then give you estimates, first of all, of the processing parameters you should use and what they think the likely outcome will be as a powder property. It is sufficiently impertinent then to tell you, in fact, you do not want properties like that. If the Expert System had run it, it would not have started where you are starting. It will also tell you, of course, that although these parameters look good, in their experience, that produces sticky powder that the housewife will not like.

You can really get quite a lot into an Expert System and far better than what we had and what preceded it, manuals—on one side equipment specification sheets telling you how to build a tower, and then process specifications which tell you how to run it. These Expert Systems are a lot more fun and certainly convey a lot more data. We hope one day we can bring all the expertise of our operators up to that of the best one in the system around the world. We have more than 50 spray drying towers, and we would really like all the operators to be of an exemplary standard.

That is one kind of Expert System—an Expert System for experts. We are at the moment developing another experiment in Colworth which is one of our food laboratories. We are developing an Expert System for line operatives, who may run the fish finger line in Birds Eye or the Lux toilet bar line in Lever Brothers. The idea again is to replace manuals and local instruction with a computer system. In this case, we are trying to provide not just start-up/shut-down or fault diagnosis programs, in the way that we do on the Expert Systems for spray drying towers. We are trying to provide for people a visual record of what they have to do on the line, how to start it up, and how to do the fault diagnosis. We are using a very simple system, which is a small IBM PC, the Sony Disc Video, and some software which we can buy off the shelf. We hope to put together a system that the operator will find more engaging than the manual which tends to be left in the office or in the shed and is rarely brought out. We hope this will encourage an operator to want to achieve better practice.

The interesting thing about this is, that if you see some of our modern factories, where there are two or three operators in a giant hall full of lines packing a range of products, the operator will be able to actually look at the video, test his problem on another person talking back to him, and in fact, he will be able to ask questions, develop plans, and so on. We think that this could be quite a useful development in having better conditions and maintenance on our production lines, apart from having the other more profound Expert Systems for the very difficult and tricky operations.

Another key area for upgrading our information system is on product information. The traditional formulation sheets are actually being displaced by a computer system which does not just give you the formulation, but advises you on the cost and the usage of raw materials, or how to substitute one component for another. It will tell you whether those ingredients have got safety clearance in the centre, because, of course, one cannot afford to put any deleterious material into a formulation. Then, it will tell you what the uses are in other countries, so the formulation designer can find out what others are doing in Malaysia or Japan or in the US—often of interest to the local application. It really is a multi-dimensional, multi-national information system which gives real benefit to the development scientist and on-line manager alike.

Overall, then we are progressing intentionally slowly, and building computer analogues which build on and improve upon the best human systems we have developed. We are doing this to achieve better performance, of course. We are achieving cost savings and people efficiencies *en route*, and we are developing people and engaging their commitment in a totally new way, at all levels. But it is only a tentative start.

Experience of IT innovation in ICI

DEREK SEDDON

I come from a commercial background, and when I was appointed Group Director for Information Technology my reaction was 'Why me?'. At that time ICI was re-evaluating a number of central activities like research, engineering, and Information Technology. One conclusion was that Information Technology is clearly going to be one of the technologies that a company like ICI had to come to grips with. The surest way of doing that was by giving someone the job of working out a strategy and sending him away to make it happen. I came into this job knowing little about Information Technology, but given the job of putting together a strategy.

I would like to talk about the experience we have had in ICI of developing an Information Technology strategy and of innovative use of the technology within our different business areas.

To put it into perspective with the earlier account from Unilever, I should note the many similarities between ICI and Unilever: our turnover is not dissimilar, we have about half the number of staff worldwide, we operate in a large number of countries and with a large number of businesses.

My job as Group Director of Information Technology is to be aware of all the opportunities and applications across the group, and ensure that we are cross-fertilizing, and that we are aware of what is going on in other companies and where the frontiers of the technology are.

I have been very much concerned about how ICI is adopting the technology, exploiting it in the key areas of research, manufacturing and in the commercial area. I hope to give you a view of the problems we have had in doing this. These problems relate to social attitudes, organization, politics, and to Information Technology itself. I would like to start by putting the social and economic environment in context for ICI.

For ICI, 1980 was something of a watershed. In that year, for the first time in our history, we made a loss in one quarter, and so it was a pretty rude awakening. There was a recognition that the sort of forces acting on the markets in which we were operating had, for perhaps the last 200 years, been largely ones of integration and standardization, but that we are now into a world in which the very opposite was occurring. We now had to cope with diversity and uncertainty. The key things that we had to be able to handle in our business and products were diversity and uncertainty; it was no longer possible to be sure that oil prices would remain fairly constant and that the economics of massive single stream integrated plants would ensure survival in the world chemical industry.

Our profit performance caused a shock in the system which led to a reappraisal of what we were trying to do in business terms. We had to assess how we were organized to handle these issues and we recognized that Information Technology was one of the key technologies for managing diversity and uncertainty.

I find it very useful to try and classify the application of technology into three broad bands.

1. *Efficiency*: where the application of the technology is really aimed at improving the efficiency of a clerical or machine activity.

2 *Effectiveness*: where it is concerned with the effectiveness of the decision making processes.

3 *Competitive advantage*: where Information Technology could actually begin to give competitive advantage.

Computers have traditionally been used, certainly in ICI, for the classic data processing of accounts, payroll, and order processing. That is where our computer experience over the last 20 years has been concentrated. During the last 7 years we have seen more and more applications giving enquiry access to data bases and using information to improve decision making processes. In the last 2–3 years we have seen several examples of companies using the technology to fundamentally change the way they do business.

In the research field you can see the application of computing to molecular modeling and statistical dynamics. It really changes the way we do research. Chemists no longer beaver away at a work bench where they try a thousand and one compounds: they use computer models. If you obtain very powerful computational equipment, you can improve the productivity of research by several orders of magnitude. If you can do that ahead of all your competitors, then you are going to gain some competitive advantage.

The real concerns that I have are:

'Are we aware of all the opportunities?'
'Are we taking all the opportunities?'
'Are we applying them effectively to enable our research capability to gain advantage rather than just to speed up some laboratory process?'

That is the spectrum over which I have been looking.

Dramatic changes in the use of Information Technology are taking place in manufacturing industry, particularly in the scheduling of engineering design and production. Instead of taking 6 months or a year to get through from design to a prototype, you can now, using IT, do it in weeks, if not days. We are seeing massive Information Technology investment in engineering and other industries, so as to improve the way product and process design is integrated.

In the commercial area you can see applications of information technology used to improve the linkages with customers; to build relationships that will help to form new strategic alliances with customers. This represents a fundamental shift in the way in which technology will affect our business. It will be important in determining how ICI will survive and prosper. In the past we tended to look at IT in this area in a traditional data processing manner. It was very much 'How could we standardize and improve the efficiency of data processing?' We have now started to look at means of handling diversity and uncertainty, and of using Information Technology in an integrated fashion to improve our competitive position.

In the literature there has been interesting and important work concerning what is popularly called 'the second industrial revolution'. Futurologists believe that we have now reached an economic watershed, that the economics of mass production have become self-destroying, because there are no longer enough markets to sustain mass production. Therefore, they predict you have to go for diversity, producing products that meet a diverse market, and manufacture the varieties that customers want. The key technology has changed: whereas in the first industrial revolution the key technology was mass production, in the second they talk of 'flexible specialization', that is, producing economically small quantities with enormous variety.

Analyses have been made of the way the different social and economic structures of America, Japan, Germany, France, Italy, and Belgium might cope with the Second Industrial Revolution. Significantly, such analyses often exclude the United Kingdom. It is as if these experts have almost written us off as being unable to compete in this new race.

On this account the Italians apparently have a social structure which, over many years, has encouraged flexible specialization. An example is the textile industry, which flourishes in Italy, but in the UK has almost been entirely destroyed by the influx of cheap Far Eastern products. Why does Italy prosper? One explanation is that they have long had small family units, surviving by living on their wits, having to continually innovate, to produce products that the market wanted, being close up against the market and responding.

This analysis also suggests that the Japanese social and economic structures are pretty well suited to this second industrial revolution. If you look at, for example, machine tools, the relationship between the motor industry and the suppliers always forced the suppliers to be innovative, to seek new technology which would allow them to improve quality and reduce costs. So innovation has been built into their culture.

The Germans have very good technical education and are said to be very quick to adapt to new technology. The American complaint was that they were slow to take up technology. My concern is that, within the UK companies, up-take of Information Technology is disturbingly inadequate.

If we are going to use Information Technology to maximum effect, both as a competitive weapon within our own industry and by UK industry in global markets, then there are some fundamental issues that have to be faced concerning innovation. We must look at the rate at which we learn to employ new ideas and use them competitively in world markets. My concern is 'How well is ICI picking up the opportunities and using them?'. The answer is 'Not as well as I would like', but maybe I am over ambitious.

I would like to address some of the management of change problems that we have encountered in IT innovation. The problem of innovation in science and technology has been around a long time and a literature has developed. It is worth repeating the old adage, that history teaches nothing, because innovation and the adoption of new technology has been a problem in the UK for as long as anyone can remember. The four key elements needed for successful innovation have been well reported, but we seem to forget them regularly.

1. You need a champion, someone who will protect and support

an innovative idea because, almost by definition, it will threaten the status quo in an organization. There is a lot of conservatism in any organization that wants to protect what exists; therefore, innovation is usually stifled at birth. The champion provides the umbrella of support.

2. You need to listen to the market, and I think that is crucial. It means 'Get feedback'. Do not presume to know what your customer needs; be that an internal or external customer. You must put in place mechanisms which take an idea to the customer, see how he reacts and then feed back the response, i.e. close the feedback loop and modify. Recent research shows that over 80 per cent of successful IT innovation usually comes from market adjustment. We forget that at our peril.

3. The other element in terms of IT is 'Limit the risk'. Extend from well known systems with new technology, or well known technology with new information, but do not try and go for new technology with new information, otherwise you double your risk.

4. The last key is a new venture mentality or, in my words, 'Be prepared to buck the system'. You must find people who are challenging, who will actually go outside the existing organizational structures.

We have experienced problems in innovation, which is about the management of change, but I do not think that they are new to IT. Nor do I think they are new to industry in the UK. They are typical of the problems that any organization faces. In working with management teams, I now construct a 2 × 2 'MANAGEMENT STYLE' matrix by seeking answers to questions such as:

Y-axis: 'What is the management's motivation for change?' i.e. 'How well motivated are managers in terms of always looking for innovation?'

and rate them from low to high, and

X-axis: 'How much pain are they experiencing in the business or the area that they are responsible for?' i.e. 'What do they perceive to be the need to actually change?'

and rate them from low to high.

The classification that I would use is as follows. If you find a management that has low perceived pain and low motivation for change, then I define this quadrant as a *complacent* group. Low pain and high motivation for change: that is my definition of an *innovative* group. If they are feeling pain and are looking for new ideas they are a pretty *hungry* management group. If they have high pain, but are not looking for change they are *tired*.

I normally ask a management group I'm about to start work with to carry out a self-analysis of their *management style*. I was dealing with a group that in my book were clearly *tired*, and it was pointed out to me by the General Manager that, in fact, there was another way of looking at the chart. The manager said my analysis was clearly wrong. The group I called *complacent*, seen from his perspective, was *efficient*. Risk-takers are often merely *flighty*; who in their right mind brings change for the sake of change? They are a risk to the organization. My *hungry* group are not so much hungry, but *desperate*. His own people were not *tired*, but *misunderstood*. I think that characterizes the problem we have with innovation: there are many different ways of looking at the same problem through different bifocals. Depending on your perspective you can say that innovation is desirable or undesirable!

I have described these problems as I see it in ICI, but I do not think it is special to ICI. I think you will find it in most UK organizations. It seems to me that the UK has a particular problem related to our social attitudes which has developed over many years.

I would like to quote here from a recent report by the IT 86 Committee—set up under the auspices of the DTI—which again is pointing out that the UK is not responding to the challenge of technical innovation:

The United Kingdom proportion of world trade has been in decline for many years. It has become accepted that the 'sunset' industries have had to decline in the face of changes in demand and capacity worldwide and the disparate costs of labour between a welfare state and most third world economies. But even in the fields of modern technology the UK is not maintaining its position despite its education system and its comparatively high investment levels in research and development.

We do not appear to be taking advantage of Information Technology. The document goes on to propose what the UK has to do to come to grips with IT in order to maintain our competitive position in world markets.

I look at history in order to learn many lessons. Here is almost the same message, but with a different time scale. A quotation from Richard Cobden, dated 1835:

Our only chance of national prosperity lies in the timely remodelling of our system, so as to put it as nearly as possible on an equality with the improved managment of the Americans.

In 1851, the peak of Britain's industrial power, Dr. Lyon Playfair wrote his book *Industrial Instruction on the Continent* which pointed out that European Industry was bound to overtake Britain if she failed to alter her outlook and methods. The Royal Commission in 1868 found that we were very deficient in general and technical education:

Unless we remedy this want we shall gradually, but surely find that our undeniable superiority in wealth and perhaps in energy will not save us from decline.

In the same year a House of Commons Select Committee report on scientific instruction reported in detail on how our professional and technical ignorance at all levels of British Industry was already beginning to rot British Industrial supremacy at its roots.

In the 1870s and 1880s there were more Royal Commissions, and in the 1890s and 1900s British defeats in world markets for want of technology and professionally qualified personnel brought to public attention by various popular campaigns, including an 1894 bestseller *British Industries and Foreign Competition*, pointing out again that Britain was not adapting, was not innovating with technology.

In 1909, there was a report from the Board of Education that should interest the educational specialists. It pointed out that, in fact, we were still not learning any lessons from the past, and that our technical education and our education of adolescents was still woefully inadequate. Following the 1914–18 war there was a special investigation to find how German industry managed how to work in the war effort, and again there was the same conclusion.

We have looked at our failure to adopt technology time and time again, and we have come to the same conclusions. So, what is going to be different with Information Technology in 1980, 1990, or 2000? Here is the challenge. It causes me great concern in terms of wanting to live in this country, yet seeing it in slow continuous decline.

Perhaps the largest and most exhaustive of all investigations into British industrial failings took place in 1924–29, when the Balfour Committee reported:

Before British industries taken as a whole can hope to reap from scientific research the full advantage which it appears to yield to some of their formidable trade rivals, nothing less than a revolution is needed in their general outlook on science.

And so it goes on. In Britain the cult of the practical man is at the heart of our outlook on life, as is the cult of the gifted amateur. How many times have we proudly heard that the gifted amateur is a characteristic of Britain.

In more recent times the Finneston report, the Alvey report, the After Alvey report, and the Bide report have all expressed similar messages to the Balfour Committee and earlier reports.

One of the most depressing books, which sums this all up and makes you wonder where we go with IT is written by Corelli Barnett. Entitled *The Audit of War*, it shows how much of our present failings have resulted from the values built into our social and economic systems. Barnett concludes that the dream of a new Jerusalem for Britain—of a socially just society—was turning into 'a dank reality of a segregated, sub literate, unskilled, unhealthy and institutionalized proletariat hanging on the nipple of state materialism.'

I am concerned at the slow rate at which ICI is taking up this technology. I believe we are certainly at the frontiers of innovation in IT in this country, but our rate of uptake is nowhere near fast enough. We are seeking to institutionalize IT in our organization, so that employees at every level are all looking to exploit the technology to maximum commercial and technical advantage. Our approach is still too traditional and not everyone shares my view of how Information Technology can revolutionize the work place and the way we compete.

I was fascinated to hear of the Unilever well structured ability to exchange technical information across the group. One of ICI's experiences is that people tend to hold on to information, seeing it as their power base, and are usually very reluctant to implement systems which share that information.

I certainly see Information Technology as critical: a technology that could revolutionize the place of ICI, (and of the UK), in world competitive markets, but I am concerned that the UK, as a country, and ICI, as a company, are not actually exploiting it as effectively as we might.

4 Directions for research and development

Directions for Information Technology research and development

DEREK BARKER

Perhaps it is rather surprising that somebody from BP should be talking about the directions Information Technology research and development might take. At first glance, it may not be obvious why an oil company is involved in this activity. However, the oil industry is a major user of IT; for example, we use advanced computer systems to help in many facets of our business, including oil reservoir modelling, and we also for example, make use of remotely operated vehicles to inspect the underwater parts of North Sea oil rigs. It is primarily because of this involvement as a major user of IT that we are interested in the directions IT developments may take, and it is also from this perspective that we are actively involved in a substantial research and development programme at our Sunbury-on-Thames Research Centre.

At present, the non-Communist world's IT industry turnover (excluding telecommunications) is about half that of its oil industry. By the end of the century it is thought that world revenues from IT will exceed those from oil (the financial aspects are outlined in Table 4.1). Clearly, no major company can afford to ignore an industry of this scale, and especially when it is likely to impact to an ever-increasing degree on our own business activities. Optimum application of IT will become a major factor in determining the competitive strength of a company in the 1990s.

But what exactly do we mean by Information Technology? Figure 4.1 lists some of the main areas embraced by this umbrella term. As can be seen, there are a number of activities which fall under this heading, and these separate areas interact in a complex manner. Clearly, the scope is enormous and we considered it essential to be

Table 4.1 IT in the world

Total research and development spend worldwide 1983	£123 000 m
IT research and development spend worldwide	£15 000 m
USA	£7 000 m
IBM	£2 100 m
Oil majors research and development	£2 400 m
Alvey Programme	£350 m over 5 years

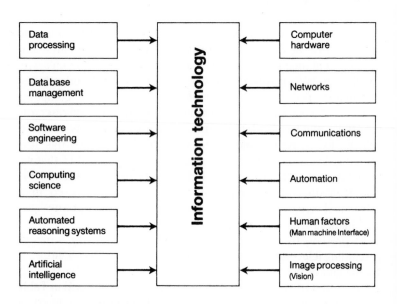

Fig. 4.1 The domain of IT.

selective in deciding which parts of the large diverse field we would concentrate on in establishing our own research and development programme. Except, perhaps, for the very largest enterprises totally involved in the IT business, it is not sensible to attempt to cover the whole field with any hope of achieving success. Selectivity and marshalling adequate resources to crack problems in specific areas are essential for success, in our view.

This may be an appropriate time to point out that there is a major problem of definitions in this field. An example concerns the term Artificial Intelligence (AI), which is very widely referred to, especially by those seeking funding for expensive research projects (reference to AI is thought by some to be worth 50 per cent more on a research grant). There is no consensus over a precise definition, however. Figure 4.2 shows some of those commonly met—I personally like Professor Brady's dictum 'Intelligent connection of perception to action'. This confusion over definitions is endemic in such a rapidly advancing field, but it unfortunately has undesirable effects such as interfering with communication, and it also, sadly, reflects muddled thinking by some of the practitioners in the field itself.

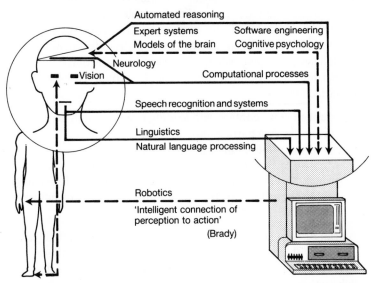

Fig. 4.2 The domain of artificial intelligence.

What then is BP's standpoint on IT research and development? The key reason for our interest is that we are coming increasingly to appreciate the central importance of IT to much of our operations, from exploring for and producing crude oil, through refining and product distribution, to marketing and selling our products to customers. We acknowledge that the suppliers of hardware and software often provide good solutions to our problems. However, we have also learned that sometimes we face problems so specialized that cost-effective solutions are not available, or problems whose solution demands an effective integration between various different technologies (e.g. IT skill and specialist applications knowledge) and which no supplier has or is likely to be able to provide. Another possibility is where we want to have a solution which is not available to our competitors. Or again, in some areas we wish to increase the effectiveness of suppliers' offerings by linking them into an existing framework such as making use of existing databases. For these and other reasons it was decided to establish some 18 months ago an IT research activity within our research and development laboratories at Sunbury. The aim is to access the best research expertise (often in universities) in selected areas, to develop this expertise along with our own fundamental advances, by means of applied research projects which will focus on applications relevant to BP's interests, and to help develop and apply solutions to operational problems throughout BP. Last, but not least, we aim to provide a steady stream of skilled people to help with implementation of the outcomes of the research and development across the BP group. These aims are summarized below.

(1)   establish close contact with leading edge research activities in universities, via participation in research clubs, etc.
(2)   establish in-house fundamental research activities.
(3)   establish 'driver' projects to focus research and development on activities where research success is of substantial advantage.
(4)   implement technology transfer by staff transfer, joint activities, and so on.

As can be seen, an essential ingredient is to establish effective co-operation with research groups in universities and elsewhere. This is easier said than done. A *sine qua non* in our view is that true collaboration is desirable and can only be achieved if both parties expect to benefit thereby. A particular need in any collaborative venture, and especially one involving technology transfer is to minimize interface problems such as those between:

(1)   universities and industrial research and development;
(2)   fundamental research and applied development;
(3)   research and development generally and commercial applications.

These interface problems can be minimized and technology also successfully transferred at each step by judicious use of staff transfer mechanisms and as secondments of industrial staff into an academic environment and vice versa, as well as sending research staff into a business operational area.

I have dwelt at some length on the reasons why BP is involved in IT research and development and what we are doing to ensure that our involvement is as effective as possible. This is because the direction we have followed is one we see as becoming more general over the next 5 years or so—that is an increasing involvement of 'users' in the development of state of the art IT systems, and in cases like our own, an active involvement will frequently be in the context of collaboration with suppliers, and will be primarily aimed at increasing the efficiency and effectiveness of the user's own business. However, an inevitable result will be that users will start to sell solutions initially developed for their own needs to other users, and this development will result in a change, possibly a profound one, in the nature of the IT market. No longer will there be a simple division into suppliers and users, but a mingling of the two activities will increasingly lead to hybrid organizations. Caveat the simple IT-cloistered suppliers!

I will now consider some of the key areas of IT research activity and outline some major lines of development which we anticipate over the coming few years. First let us consider image processing/vision systems. This is a particularly active area, and one which is at the beginning of a major period of development in my view. Images are fundamental to many of the things we do; they are one of the most widely encountered forms in which data is acquired, stored and presented by humans, but not so far by computers. Why not? One of the key problems is the difficulty of storing images in a compact digital form, which is somewhat ironical: a picture is worth a thousand words, but also demands a million pixels (just for one picture!). If I say 'There is a yellow car parked on a busy road with a blue lorry parked next to it', in a matter of eighteen words I have conveyed a huge quantity of information which can be employed to form a picture in the mind's eye. How does one store that quantity of information in a computer? The human mind can compress visual data very effectively indeed, way beyond that achievable as yet in a machine. A sidelight on the frustration felt by many is that humans handle visual information in a very sophisticated manner, and it sometimes comes as a surprise to find the lamentably primitive state of digital image storage and processing! An example of this is Fig. 4.3: with a little effort most people can recognize a dog sniffing

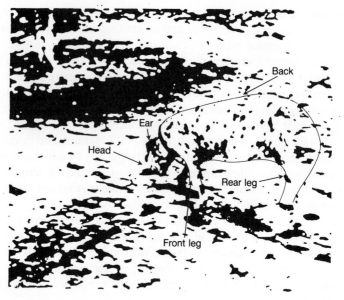

Fig. 4.3 'Spot the dog'.

among fallen leaves; to a computer it is just so many black and white areas and probably nothing more.

Key research questions in this field include:

(1)   What gives things their appearance?
(2)   How can multiple images be used to best effect?
(3)   How should image features be best represented in a digital system?
(4)   How can 3-D information be recovered from 2-D images?
(5)   How can we design a digital system which recognizes individual objects, its location and orientation with respect to those objects, and which can then navigate around them quickly and successfully?

Two examples of potential applications of image processing/vision systems within BP may be of interest. The first is the use of multiple image processing procedures to progressively 'home-in' a remotely operated vehicle (ROV) on a subsea structure, e.g. for maintenance. The ROV will generally use sonar sensors in order to navigate to within (murky) visual range of the desired part of the structure. If cleaning of the structure is then required, the visibility may well be so impaired by the debris resulting from this operation that subsequent movement to a closely adjoining location might well have to rely on tactile sensors. Effective integration of information from a variety of sensors of this nature is a difficult research target and beyond the competence of current state-of-the-art systems.

A second potential application is artificial colour enhancement of video images of flames. In a furnace, such as those in distillation units or other refinery plant, the shape and brightness of the various parts of a flame is an indicator of burner performance. Unfortunately, the naked eye can only pick up relatively large departures from the 'correct' flame characteristics. However, images of a flame obtained via a video camera can be subject to synthetic colour enhancement, the various parts of the flame being shown in different colours, in line with subtle differences in brightness which cannot be detected by the eye, and the resulting image projected onto a screen. Operators can then detect even small departures from ideal functioning of the burner (see Fig. 4.4). Clearly, such a system could be linked with an Expert System which would provide advice to operators on the correct remedial action, based on analysis of the flame shape and relative brightness of its various parts. This illustrates another trend in IT—the linking together of separate systems into an integrated system; regrettably, this is easier said than done as anyone who has attempted to make one computer talk to another can testify.

Talking of integrated systems leads me to refer to an important area of research which some people regard as the most important topic in IT developments—this is the use of 'natural language interfaces'. Usually, this is taken to mean the ability to instruct a computer by speaking to it; there is a considerable amount of research underway in this area, but I have to admit that the results so far are disappointing in that commercially available systems are very limited in the size of vocabulary they can handle, have frequently to be 'taught' to recognize each user's pronunciation, and are error-prone. One of the major difficulties is that words mean different things depending on the particular context in which they are used. This ambiguity can be illustrated by two examples. Figure 4.5 shows an 'intelligent' lawnmower, but does 'a longer lawn' mean the grass is taller or the length of the lawn is greater? The second example is a joke: two ladies arrive for lunch at a Gentlemens' Club (presumably in a less advanced society than ours), and are told by the head waiter that only gentlemen are served. To which they reply 'Splendid; bring us two immediately!'.

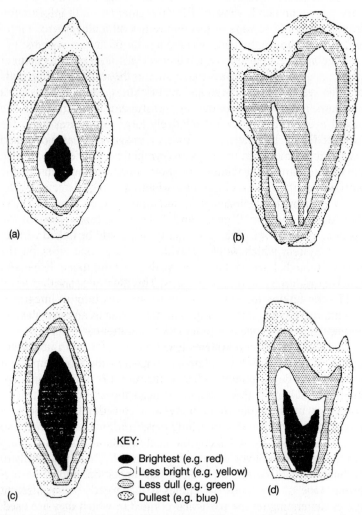

Fig. 4.4 Representation of video images of flames with synthetic colour enhancement. (a) Normal flame (15 per cent excess air). (b) Insufficient air (8 per cent excess air). (c) Too much air (40 per cent excess air). (d) Blocked jet.

'The trouble is, it's been programmed to cut a longer lawn.'

Fig. 4.5 Natural language problems.

Despite all the difficulties, it will be surprising if reasonably capable natural language processors do not emerge over the next five or so years; they will probably depend on parallel processors to give the necessary speed and vocabulary/context handling capability. If I am right, this development could lead to a major boost in the use of computers because it will remove the irksome need to input data and instructions through a keyboard, which many potential users find unacceptable.

No one can talk about future directions in IT research and development without mentioning Expert Systems. In some ways this is a pity because whilst Expert Systems are an area of considerable research and development activity, and they do offer exciting potential in many application areas; the plain truth is that they have been oversold too often for the good of the technology. This over-hyping leads to expectant users becoming disillusioned when the anticipated performance is not obtained and the end-result is that the technology as a whole becomes discredited. Currently available Expert Systems can tackle certain classes of problems, usually those of limited size, where the variables are precisely quantifiable and well-bounded. Used in appropriate circumstances, these are quite useful and satisfactory. However, the major problems which my company, and many others, would like to attack with help from Expert Systems are frequently ill-defined, non-quantitative in nature, and there is no well-recognized source of expertise available. Substantial technical hurdles need to be overcome if such problems are to be tackled. Some of the difficult areas are how to acquire expertise efficiently from either many experts, or none; and how to store this expertise efficiently in a digital system and how to access it quickly and flexibly; how to make maximum effective use of pre-existing data stored in data bases; and how to represent fuzzy or imprecise reasoning (such as 'If the car starts to drift to the right, apply left hand down a bit'). Only when these and other problems are satisfactorily overcome will Expert Systems come of age, in my view. This will demand substantial research and development effort, and regrettably the number of skilled practitioners in this field being turned out by UK educational institutions is smaller than I would like to see. We are at a significant disadvantage because of this small skills base, and in danger of waking up one day in 1991 to find the field has been conquered by the Americans.

From this gloomy picture I would like to end on a much more positive picture. This concerns the major shift which is likely to take place in the methods used to construct computer programmes. Software development with the methods currently used to build programs is rather akin to a cottage or craft industry—it is labour intensive; the techniques are not automated to any significant extent; the results are often short on reliability and long on cost. At present, for example, the cost of program maintenance can amount to two-thirds of the total cost of a program. However, a significant change is likely to take place over the coming few years. This 'software engineering' revolution will lead to a much more automated, reliable, and lower cost program production method, and the resulting programs will be much more what the user wants, and more easily capable of modification or updating in line with his changing requirements subsequently. The movement towards this mecca is based on use of rigorous application of mathematical techniques and logical transformations, capable of being proved to be consistent from one step to another throughout the process of producing a program. To show how these developments will impact on the nature and cost of program production, let us look at three block-flow diagrams (Figs 4.6–8). In each case they show the major steps

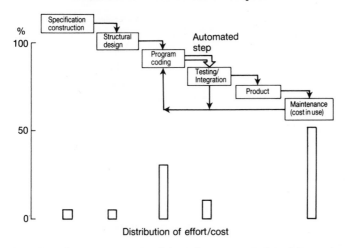

Fig. 4.6 Software engineering life cycle: current industrial practice.

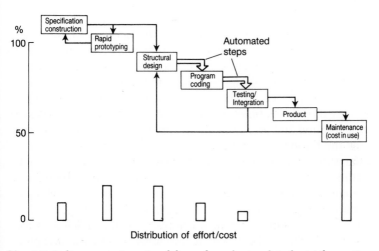

Fig. 4.7 Software engineering life cycle: advanced industrial practice now being introduced (20 per cent cost reduction).

involved together with the proportionate cost of each step, and the total cost, in the form of bars along the bottom of each figure. Figure 4.6 shows the current process; as can be seen, there are a number of steps, only one of which is (even partly) automated; modifications to the program resulting from testing, user's reaction, or maintenance needs are inherently complex and costly because they attempt to

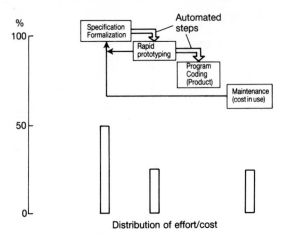

Fig. 4.8 Software engineering life cycle: research prototype 1991 (90 per cent cost reduction).

modify the completed program, and the majority of the cost is incurred in the later stages of the programming cycle. Apart from its sheer inefficiency, this approach cannot fail to upset the users.

The second figure shows the best current industrial practice. More effort is expended in the earlier stages, on activities such as specification development and prototyping potential solutions to get user reaction and also to guide the programmers themselves as to how the finished program will behave. This approach is likely to offer some improvement in performance and reliability over the traditional techniques, and the overall cost is likely to be reduced, perhaps by up to 20 per cent. However, this is only scratching the surface of what will become possible if the work going on in universities and other research centres bears the anticipated fruit. Figure 4.7 shows the result of this move towards a disciplined 'engineering' approach based on sound and rigorous theoretical foundations. Here, the initial stage, that of developing a formal specification using mathematical notation, absorbs a much greater proportion of the total effort. This specification can be rapidly and cheaply translated into a prototype solution, and when the latter has been optimized to meet the user's needs, the code writing will be effected automatically using computer programs which will actually write other programs. Although maintenance cannot be eliminated, the reliability of the finished program will be much higher than is the norm today, and the cost and difficulty of effecting modifications and updates will be greatly diminished. The overall cost of the program will be reduced by an order of magnitude or more.

How will this come about? Well, there has been a lot of fundamental research effort in universities and elsewhere for several years, and this has led to a number of competing methods for attacking many of the parts of the total program production process. What is now needed is to develop these techniques further, and integrate them into coherent methodologies able to address the whole production process. Then these methodologies will be tested on trial problems of progressively increasing size and complexity. Winners and losers will thus emerge.

I said I would end on a high note. This is that in this field of software engineering at least, the UK has a substantial fraction of the worldwide expertise. This is a good position to be in; what we must ensure is that the profitable commercial application of this expertise is something in which the UK retains its lead. BP is intent on doing its part in ensuring that this and other IT developments are applied to the benefit of the company and the country.

Expert Systems—where do we go from here?

JOHN TAYLOR

Introduction

The purpose of this talk is to provide some perspectives on how Expert Systems are likely to develop over the next 10 years or so. The terms of reference for this part of the seminar seem to imply that this should be done by surveying the research scene, and then doing some extrapolation and some synthesis. However, as the fields of Expert System and knowledge-based programming research have emerged from their parent endeavour of Artificial Intelligence research over the past 10–20 years, they have developed a very significant distinguishing characteristic. This is the shift away from trying to build machines with some aspect of general human intelligence and towards building increasingly powerful knowledge-based tools which people can use to help them solve quite specific types of problems in quite specific domains. Indeed, many would argue that it is this relatively modest and pragmatic emphasis on applications and usefulness to the end-user that has facilitated much of the real theoretical progress that research has made in the last decade.

Accordingly, in considering what progress is likely in the field of expert systems in 10 years time, I believe it is important to look beyond the foreseeable achievements of current research activities to understand something about the pressures and imperatives that will guide the research, and set priorities for investment of talent as it proceeds.

These pressures seem to be of at least three distant kinds.

(1) Success: if research in some topic is going very well, keep pushing.
(2) User needs: what kind of systems do applications and end users really want?
(3) Progress in related fields: radical improvements in cost/performance microelectronics, communications, displays, and so on.

In the Information Systems Lab in Bristol, we have found it quite helpful in formulating our research priorities to focus discussion around two key questions.

(1) What kind of systems would end-users really like to have 5–10 years hence and why can't we build them now?
(2) How will foreseeable technology research and development change the kinds of system we can build?

In this talk, I propose to use a similar approach. That is, I want to discuss some key attributes which I believe will characterize Expert Systems 10 years on; to show that these are indeed consonant with some of our current mainstream research directions; and finally, to sketch what this may mean from the viewpoint of the user's world a decade hence.

Let me begin, though, by saying a few words about what current expert systems are and what they are not.

Current Expert Systems

I have no need or intention of providing here any kind of state-of-the-art review, since I am sure this will have been covered extensively in other sessions. However, in order to see more clearly what research must achieve if we are to have the kinds of systems we shall be discussing later, it will be helpful to summarize a few points about current expert systems.

Present Expert Systems are essentially *classifiers* written using knowledge-based programming techniques. More specifically an Expert System obtains some data from its user about the particular case under consideration, usually by some dialogue process. It then carries out a classification or categorization of the data according to internally stored knowledge which may be of various kinds (e.g. factual, procedural, causal) held in a variety of possible representations (e.g. rules, frames, semantic networks). This classification process is achieved by applying some appropriate set of inference procedures to the knowledge base, which culminates in presenting one or more results (diagnoses, classification, etc) to the user.

Associated with these there are often appropriate courses of action and the system is usually able to offer an 'explanation' of the conclusion, often in the form of a summary of the inference steps it went through to achieve it.

This basic 'classification' paradigm is, of course, quite limited, but it is surprisingly powerful and can be effective in a wide variety of tasks, from diagnosis of faults and diseases to identification of promising geological features to speech understanding. When applied in the form of 'critiquing' it can be even more generally useful, e.g. in advising on the various merits or otherwise of a proposed plan of action.

Now let us consider what current Expert Systems are *not*.

Firstly, even in the limited domains where current expert systems have achieved some limited success, they do not replace human experts in the sense of making them no longer necessary. This is for two reasons.

(1) The human expert is necessary to help build the knowledge base in the first place.
(2) The human expert is necessary to keep the knowledge base up to date as the nature of the task, the domain and our knowledge of it changes with time, as they inevitably will.

The areas of knowledge elicitation, knowledge representation, knowledge acquisition, and machine learning are still in their infancy, and so the knowledge-base of a typical Expert System of today is still very much a hand-crafted set of perhaps at most a few thousand items (facts, rules, etc.) specially built for that one specific task and domain. It is not in any useful sense general or generally applicable knowledge, and it is not capable of modifying or extending itself in the light of performance or experience. Current Expert Systems have their main value therefore not in replacing human experts, which they cannot do, but in making their more routine expertise in a particular task more widely available, usually to people less specialized in that particular area (e.g. fault diagnosis for technicians, equipment configuration for salesmen, disease diagnosis for general practitioners).

Secondly, despite all the hype to the contrary, present Expert Systems are not particularly friendly, much less intelligent, to the user. This is primarily because their knowledge of the domains of the problem, or the task, is still at a very shallow or superficial level, and this greatly restricts the kinds of problem solving activity and the kinds of dialogue they can support.

Finally, current expert systems are not particularly cheap, either to produce, to deliver or to maintain, and in areas such as documentation and acceptance testing there is still great scope for progress.

Expert Systems of the future

Having summarized why today's Expert Systems represent a promising first step in the application of knowledge-based programming ideas in building tools to help people solve problems, let us now look at where the road might lead over the next decade or so.

In considering the kinds of systems we would really like to be able to build 10 years from now, I believe we can distinguish three main attributes.

Knowledge base management

We will move from small, hand-crafted special-purpose knowledge bases to large assemblages of knowledge which can be used by a wide variety of different application systems for many different purposes.

This trend, we believe will be inevitable because the investment and commitment required from an organization to acquire large amounts of explicit knowledge in machine-based form mean that such knowledge must be made generally available and useable to a wide range of applications over a long period of time. There is a close analogy with 'conventional' programming where small stand-alone programs can have their own, private hand-crafted data representations, but where large, evolving, multi-application systems require the use of explicit data base management systems.

These allow important data to be structured and managed independently of any particular application and maintained as one of the key long-term assets of an organization. Accordingly, we refer to 'knowledge base management systems' and the development of KBMS technology will require much progress in our understanding of ideas of structure, modularity, and hierarchy in large, complex knowledge-based systems. Again, in comparison with 'conventional' programming, these are still at an early stage, but work in a number of research laboratories including our own in Bristol look promising. Perhaps the areas of greatest difficulty will be those of knowledge elicitation and acquisition, which are in turn closely linked to representation issues. If we are to put large quantities of explicit knowledge into machine-supported forms over an extended period of time, then we will need better machine support for the acquisition process itself and we will need to organize our representations of knowledge around much deeper models and theories of the domains involved.

Co-operative problem solving

The emergence of KBMS technology has to do with enabling the investment and commitment needed to make large amounts of explicit knowledge available in machine-based form reliably. However, for this to be of any lasting value, it must be *used*, and my second key attribute of Expert Systems a decade hence is to do with making them much more *useful* than they are today. I do not believe that this will occur primarily by creating more and more powerful problem solvers for particular domains and tasks. Rather, I believe the main trend ought to be a move from today's small, specialized Expert Systems able to carry out diagnostic, classification-type tasks based on shallow knowledge optimized for a particular task, to suites of knowledge-based *consultants* able to assist people in a co-operative way to solve a wide range of problems in various domains.

These consultants systems will use the knowledge available from KBMS and other more local sources, and will be co-operative in two senses.

(1) They will co-operate with the user in a flexible dialogue where either side may have the initiative according to the needs of the problem.

(2)   They will co-operate with each other so that, for example, one may use the services of another to assist with some sub-problem.

In particular, the prime roles of these knowledge-based consultants will be:

(1)   to work with the user to help *him* to formulate his problem;
(2)   to provide useful, intelligible advice to help *him* to solve it.

Whilst these will require powerful domain problem solvers, the prime area where innovation is needed is concerned with developing much more powerful and general dialogue modes between the user and the expert.

Our research on these topics in the Bristol Research Centre envisages three main capabilities for these dialogues:

1. *Answering a range of questions*. This has to provide flexible access to the knowledge available to the system and to the user to assist the user in describing and formulating his problem, and later in understanding and evaluating possible solutions to it. The process of answering questions is essentially a problem-solving task itself. For example, today's fault diagnosis Expert Systems are usually only capable of answering two kinds of questions in rather limited ways based on their shallow knowledge of the system concerned and its environment.

(a)   What is the fault?
(b)   What is the remedy?

Their usefulness would be very greatly enhanced if they could also deal with questions like:

(a)   Why did the fault occur?
(b)   Why did the remedy work?
(c)   Why didn't the remedy work?
(d)   Will my proposed remedy work?
(e)   How can I test whether my proposed remedy will work?

This will require much deeper and more general theories and models of the domain and the environment than we have today, and these will of course also allow a corresponding expansion of the scope and power of the questions the expert systems will put to the user, compared to today's rather tedious data extraction sessions.

2. *Co-operative problem solving*. This area of dialogue is pri-marily to do with the negotiation between the system and the user of

likely solutions to the problem as formulated. It will involve the user in volunteering information that may be relevant, constraints on possible solutions, suggestions for solutions and so on. As the user and the system jointly explore the constraints on solutions, the system may also volunteer information. For example, the user may ask if X would be a viable solution:

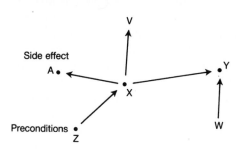

User: Will X achieve Y?
Expert: No, not unless Z becomes true beforehand.
          No, but W will.
          No, but X will achieve V instead.
          Yes, as long as Z is true.
          Yes, but so will W.
          Yes, but it will also cause A.
          Yes, because Z is true already.

3. *Describe, explain, and justify the solutions.* Having formulated the problem space and helped each other to explore the likely nature of acceptable solutions, this area of dialogue has to do with organizing and presenting the system's advice to the user, and handing the initiative back to user to make the final decisions about what to do. In particular, therefore, it is concerned with:

(1)   organizing a clear, concise, understandable presentation of the various possible solutions, plans, courses of action, etc., that they have agreed are candidates for decision;
(2)   setting out clearly a summary of the reasons why they are acceptable and the likely trade-offs and penalties involved;
(3)   spelling out any conditions, caveats, and dependencies which are essential for any particular solution to be viable.

In short, this phase provides a 'briefing document' on which the user can now make his final decisions for action, and which will serve as a record of the *outcomes* of the co-operative problem-solving consultation between the user and his expert.

Networks

The third attribute which I believe will be key to Expert Systems 10 years on is, perhaps surprisingly, not directly related to knowledge-based programming as we know it today. Computer networks today are still at a rather early, immature stage with a plethora of different systems, some standards beginning to emerge and as yet rather limited connectivity and use. In 10 years time I expect that computer networks will have got over the 'critical mass hump' as telephone networks did earlier this century, so that one can say 'most people (of interest to me) are easily available on the network'. In short, it will then be possible to go up to a workstation and be connected via a network of networks to perhaps hundreds of thousands or millions of other computers and workstations. I believe this has at least three crucial implications for future expert system developments.

1. It will enormously increase the range of knowledge-bases and expert problem solvers of all kinds that are (potentially) available to any given expert consultant system. As more and more knowledge and expertise become available in machine-based form the problem-solving power available to any individual will increase very rapidly as we begin to understand how to let individual systems co-operate.

2. It will also make the full range of 'conventional' data bases and software services available to Expert Systems' and this again will enormously enhance their capabilities compared to our current Expert Systems which tend to be 'islands of AI' with very limited access to and integration with the whole world of 'conventional' programming and services.

3. Managing the interactions between a user at his workstation and a world consisting (potentially) of millions of other machines will itself require the use of expert systems type technology, because the user's interface needs to be made very much simpler and more natural than it is even today. There are two particular directions that we in HP Laboratories are reasonably clear about at this stage:

(a) The use of Expert Systems to help manage the networks and the user's interfaces to facilities and services available on them will go hand in hand with developing better user metaphors for understanding how to use them—e.g. the various notions of 'agent' currently being researched in many laboratories.

(b) The emergence of better paradigms for thinking about how to design and program, and use components in such a huge and evolving world will derive crucially from ideas on open systems interconnection and information hiding, in which the intent is to minimise the knowledge one component needs to have about another in order to interoperate with it. Various object-oriented programming approaches seem to embody the right kind of thinking and as we begin to generalize these to fully-distributed systems and multi-vendor environments, it seems as if there may be some feasible ways ahead.

Conclusions

In highlighting three key attributes of future Expert Systems I do not mean to imply that research on other closely related areas such as natural language, vision, robotics and so on will not be important. Indeed, both in direct contribution (e.g. voice interaction in expert system consultations) or more indirectly (e.g. in contributing to our theoretical understanding of deep modelling) they will play a vital role. Likewise, dramatic progress in novel parallel architectures and languages might greatly affect the pace of the developments I have outlined, and the performance and cost improvements achieved. Other developments in fields such as displays, storage, and communications could have equally significant impacts.

However, I still believe that the overall direction of Expert Systems research in the next 10 years will be driven by those three key factors:

(1)   knowledge base management;
(2)   co-operative problem solving;
(3)   networking.

This is basically because I believe that these are fundamentally what users will require; that is, they are what we will have to do to deliver really useful services to them. This whole field of knowledge-based systems is very young and displays the characteristics of almost every major engineering discipline in its early days. We are beginning to know pragmatically how to build quite useful systems. We have as yet few general principles and very little science at all, in terms of theories which explain and predict, and so allow us to design for optimality. The next few years will therefore be a period in which the pragmatists explore potential market places and the researchers come along behind trying to do some engineering science on their successes. That which users will find really useful will thus have a dominant effect on the directions we are all able to follow.

Acknowledgements

I am grateful to my colleagues, Bill Sharpe and Alison Kidd, in the Bristol Research Centre of Hewlett–Packard Laboratories for their assistance in preparing this transcript.

5 Implications of Advanced Information Technology: a trade union view

Social effects of IT—past and future

BILL JORDAN

Our subject is really a moving target—whatever we say about it today it will probably be a bit different tomorrow. I have been in the engineering industry for well over 30 years. When I started the industry looked unchangeable and as if it had changed little in the previous 20 or 30 years. The old lathes that I used, the shapers and borers, they had always been around and looked like being around for ever. Things have certainly altered; when I was asked to discuss this subject I started to look at it and realized just how much of a newcomer I was to it. It was almost frightening to know that some of the things I have started to talk about on behalf of my members are beyond my own experience: I really have no clue about operating some of the new equipment. Industrial relations, however, is not necessarily about knowing how to operate the latest flexible manufacturing system.

Revolutions, it was said, devour their young. They also indiscriminately injure multitudes of innocent bystanders. The needless suffering that was perpetuated during the first industrial revolution spawned the modern trade union movement, and the trade union movement now watches warily and not without apprehension as the technological revolution gathers momentum. We see Information Technology in particular fuelling the pace of change to the point of it taking on the characteristics of a nuclear chain reaction, with all the same potential for benefiting society if controlled, or causing considerable damage to the stability of society and to individuals within it if unchecked. The evidence to date is that the control is being exercised through the philosophy of market forces, which are insensitive to the effects of change on people.

I would like to consider a few of the developments and trends in the world of work as they appear to us, and look at their implications for the amount of work, its nature, and its pattern (Fig. 5.1). We must consider what elements of control need to exist to make the revolution work for us and not the other way around.

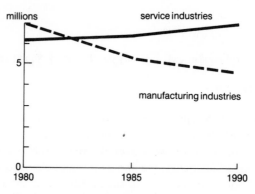

Fig. 5.1 Employment trends in service and manufacturing industries.

Perhaps the hardest pill for my union and myself to swallow is the certainty that the age of a massive manufacturing population is over. Even if the political plug that was pulled on the manufacturing industry was put back by a pro-manufacturing Labour government the shift from manufacturing to services will continue. 1960 saw 49 per cent of the working population in manufacturing and approximately 43 per cent in services. The balance has slipped so that now just about a quarter of the working population is in manufacturing, while over 60 per cent is now engaged in services. The factories of the big battalions are still crumbling.

In 1981, 60 per cent of people in private sector manufacturing were in plants with over a thousand people. My industrial relations apprenticeship was spent in one such plant, with 6000 people at one stage, when I was a full-time convenor. I got out, not on purpose, but almost by accident, into the role that I now play, but on looking back it really was a lifeboat that was passing, unbeknownst to me at that time. I now visit the remnants of that factory, and will this Christmas probably join up with one or two of my mates who also used to be there, but have not been as fortunate as I have. To my certain knowledge three of the people I will be meeting have been out of work in the $2\frac{1}{2}$ years since they left that company. All of them, regrettably, are of an unemployable age, and have skills that are not being called upon in the West Midlands.

In the next 10 years the big plants, those with over a thousand workers, are going to reduce in number. Rather than 60 per cent, I think we can look to about just over 50 per cent, and to a continued fall. Within companies, big or small, the future will see the steady, but remorseless growth of computer integrated systems. I would suggest that it is only the forces of the recession and the natural reticence of those who like to see others pay the price of experience that have steadied the spread so far. Only the big companies in America, like Boeing, have been rich enough to go the whole hog on the latest technological playthings, while the smaller fry in that country and this are content still to buy bits of this technological Lego. Jaguar, to my knowledge, boasts of its 'islands of technology', and are ready to build integrated bridges as the cash flows in. Others are purchasing piecemeal in anticipation of more prosperous times. By the year 2010 over half of all large enterprises, including services, will be using extensive integrated systems—systems of Information Technology including public and private telecommunications networks, text and data processing for offices and factories, intelligent knowledge-based systems, CAD/CAM, and other factory automation.

I think we all know that Information Technology increases the ability of large companies to operate like loose confederacies and on an international scale, while it is also facilitating the development of even larger companies in the United Kingdom. One worker in two in manufacturing now works for a multi-national. Nevertheless, the trend of the actual size of the establishments is towards smaller, but more specialized units. One motive for this, we would claim, is the breaking down of the highly unionized power of the large work-forces. It is also claimed that the enhanced capability of responding to changing market circumstances and the economies of scale are giving way to the economies of scope. A prominent role is played by compact companies with flexible manufacturing systems and machining centres that can quickly be reprogrammed to accommodate a niche in the market identified by corporate marketing resources. Such companies, of course, will in turn be increasingly sub-contracting for specialist requirements.

If technology is changing the corporation, what is it doing to the workforce? We have seen that it is shrinking in unit size. Predictions overall are for a small national workforce. As a percentage of the population by 2010 the current figure of 45 per cent is expected to be down to about 41 per cent. If Trades Unions have their way this statistic would be accommodated by an adequately funded later start to working life, by reason of a technologically extended education. Of course, we would also be advocating an earlier clocking-off at the retirement end of the career, again, adequately funded. It is this that frightens people off: the seemingly attractive proposition of early retirement. Large numbers have, in fact, gone, but do not be misled; for many of them, the company was making them an offer they knew they could not refuse. If they did not take that offer, in a year's time they could have found themselves in one of those unfortunate companies that simply collapsed without any offer of redundancy terms.

The issue of a shorter working life really ought to be tackled by the leaders of industry and commerce. We do not still need everybody serving the average of 49 years before the mast, not now that sail has given way to steam. My union has nailed its colours to the mast on the introduction of new technology: there has to be a shorter working week for those who embrace it. That is what I have been saying locally and now I am saying it nationally. The last 86 years have seen 14 hours knocked off the adult full-time worker's basic hours. With the changing pattern of work breaking the Trade Union speed limit we will not tolerate further reductions in the working week creeping at this petty pace.

Another thing is certain—the high cost of technology, with or without integration, means that more of our members will be working unsociable hours. A recent survey by the Labour Research Department shows that while only 7 per cent of companies have introduced aspects of flexitime, 49 per cent had reported changes in shift patterns. In the context of inevitable change we will be increasingly arguing for socially advantageous shift arrangements. Longer leisure breaks is one of the phrases currently used.

I personally have been involved, as a local regional official, where a group of managers were asked to go on shift. Once we had worked out a shift pattern I was asked if I would go in and get a higher premium payment for the shift. The Senior Manager I was negotiating with said: 'Come off it, Mr Jordan. You know as well as I do, they will snatch your hand off at this offer' and I said 'Well, you may be right. Perhaps we could put it to the test. I will tell you what I will do.

If *you* will offer to work this shift pattern I will accept the premium you are offering.' Well, he did not quite feel in the mood that day, so he increased the premium. When I went back to the managers concerned they said 'You did well there Bill. I think the Gaffer knew we would have worked it anyway'. They were talking about a period of continuous working, but then a whole week off, at fairly frequent intervals.

With the introduction of the longer leisure break, which may or may not be acceptable, at work or at play the composition of the workforce will change. The skilled workers clock on, the unskilled workers will clock off, and the numbers of limited skills workers will diminish. What will grow is the number of multi-skilled minders of these one-man machine shops. They are a small, but far from happy band at the moment, and it is crucial that their numbers, status, and pay grow.

It is a sick joke that we have launched into this new technological age with the most severe fall in industrial training ever experienced. It is an indictment on government and employers alike. Companies must take in the fact that the future means a permanently higher training budget. We, as Trade Unionists, have to get used to the revolutionary idea that being trained for life, which was what I was brought up to believe in, has got to give way to training through life, and that is not going to be an easy thing for our members to accept.

Those who preach and lecture about the constraints of labour must break down their status-ridden barriers to mobility. There are thousands of companies who have staff status clubs that you cannot enter if you are wearing blue overalls, and there is still a 17+ examination that decides whether you will enter the rarified environment of technician training. The greatest obstacle to change is insecurity, and the way that this transition period is handled by employers can either lay the foundations for a mature, human confidence building approach to continuous change, or be a reinforcement of the deep-down belief that history has changed nothing.

All too often there has been a vindication of those who say 'with management, profit will always take preference to people'. Change has come, unfortunately, not just at a regrettable pace, but in the most devastating way to many of our factories. At numberless meetings, shop stewards have stood up and told of the latest plight that has befallen their company, and the callous way in which it has been handled. While this goes on, the less chance we have of handling change.

We now have available in Information Technology the tools of education, the tools of persuasion. I have to tell you that those video visionaries from the lands of the Far East, the Japanese, are not yet fully locked into the potential of this persuasive force. I was on a visit to Japan, walking round the Sony factory, and was interviewing a young lady who was inspecting one of the sets as it went along the track, and was being filmed doing it. Suddenly a hooter or a buzzer went throughout the whole area; up this young lady leapt and, along with all her colleagues, literally ran. At the sight of all these Japanese workers running, I thought 'Thank God for that—a Longbridge tea break'. Then I was disillusioned—they all gathered in serried ranks at the end of each row and out came the little wooden boxes. Up stood a white-coated supervisor and, in a language I could not quite understand, started telling them all the mistakes they had made the day before. This amateurish school assembly type morning team briefing, which I know is starting to find its way here, will eventually give way to the regular rest room video presentation on every subject pertinent to prosperity: technical training, quality, the competition, and of course, the beneficial reasons for joining the AEU. All those things will be designed, to help to smooth the path of change.

Companies will be judged on the basis of how they deal with those whose skills were shaped to serve a different age, but served it well. The new technology agreements will be the manuals of change. They will not only set out the rules for catering for technological change, but they will also set out the requirements for catering for the human past.

The problems of IT and their solutions

DAVE ROGERS

I would like to explain how we have tried to manage change within my union, and to outline the developments which we have tried to bring about. It is what is a fairly simplistic approach or philosophy which we have as a union towards the introduction of new technology and towards change in general.

We know that the sort of radical and accelerating technical changes our members are being faced by now are going to create problems. It is wrong to think that we as a union are in a position to always capitalize on new technology. We have had, and continue to have, tremendous problems because of its introduction. If, for example, you look at the case of Plesseys in Edge Lane, we can remember the days when 17 000 people worked there on the manufacture of telecommunications equipment. A lot of those people were our members. The telephone equipment was very labour intensive in its production: lots and lots of bits and pieces that had to be physically screwed and soldered and bolted together. System X, the latest telephone system, is about 10 times less labour intensive than that, so the work force at that particular place has shrunk to about 2500. We know, from our experience, that the introduction of new technology and this process of rapid change will bring with it tremendous problems.

On balance, however, we are quite convinced that to ignore that technology, to put our face against such change, would create even more problems. We know that when we look to manufacturing companies overseas, in the engineering manufacturing industry or whatever, in the countries with which we are always compared, Germany, Japan, and the USA, we find that the changes we are seeing here are happening there also. In some cases these changes are happening at a far greater rate overseas than we are experiencing. It is our belief that if this trend goes on unchecked we will finish up in a less competitive position than we have now, which in the long term would be disastrous for us all.

We support whole-heartedly the ideas put forward by Bill Jordan: earlier retirement, a later start to work, and so on. Of course, such ideas can only be implemented if, first, there is the political will to bring such changes about and, secondly, if the country that wants to bring about such changes produces sufficient wealth to pay for them. That has to be our basic starting point. We support change; we believe change is inevitable; we believe that we will make more of a success of this country if we utilize change for the benefit of all. That, however, is the big problem: how do you utilize change in this way?

If we look at our membership we see that the biggest problem they have had has been in keeping up with the developments with which they are confronted. We seem to have the mentality in this country that training is a one-off event. You leave school, you do some training. For most of our members and for Bill Jordan's members, training has meant an apprenticeship. Our mentality is static: you have been trained, that is it now for 40 or 45 years. That might have been true 30 years ago, though I doubt whether it really was true even then, though you could live in industry with that philosophy. The industrial technology we are now using is no more than 7 or 8 years old. When we consider the impact computers are having in industry, we must realize that the devices either did not exist or were much simpler 7 or 8 years ago, when the first 4-bit microprocessors started to be introduced. That means, in terms of our membership, that even somebody in their mid-twenties will probably never have received any formal training on that technology. Apprenticeships, by definition, lag behind technology. Technology advances; then training managers sit down and devise a new training programme; and by the time that has all been implemented there is a time lag. We know for a fact that even members of our union in their mid-twenties have received no formal training in this technology. If you are 30 then you are getting on in life. If you are 35 you are really old, and there is really no chance of somebody that age ever having received training in the technology we are considering here, simply because it did not even exist when he was under training.

This situation has presented our members with a tremendous problem. First, there has been almost a total lack of training. Secondly, where the training did exist, and they would, of course, acknowledge that there were a few areas where the training existed, it was the wrong sort of training. I have to be very careful of what I say now in the presence of colleagues in a college of further education, and I am of course generalizing. A lot of training in our traditional technical colleges and polytechnics has tended to be far too academic for industrial uses. It tends to be taught far too mathematically, and with very little practical hands-on training. Our members are practical people. They are used to doing a practical job with tools and, unless training relates to that, they are not going to learn by it very well.

The third point made by our members is an interesting one. Many organizations, when there is an influx of new technology into their plant, cope with it by sending people away on manufacturers' training courses. These have their place, but they can, however, be bad. For example, I can quote cases where our members have been sent to Japan for a month at tremendous expense. Nobody spoke English, all the manuals were in Japanese, and they came back more confused than when they went. At best, these sort of courses do imply that the people coming on them have some fundamental knowledge of the technology. For example, let us take something like a computer numerically-controlled machine tool. A manufacturer's course on that will assume that you know what microprocessors are and how they do what they do. If you do not know that basic technology, then there is no way you will understand a manufacturer's course, so again you come back even more confused than when you left. There is a double problem associated with this because, by and large, British industry picks bright fellows to send on training courses first. If they come back confused then the entire workforce, particularly on the maintenance side, lose confidence, and if there is one problem that adults have with this technology, it is confidence. If you, as employers or lecturers, do anything to shake what little confidence people have in their own ability with this technology, then the result is disastrous. We must encourage our members to understand that new technology is not magic and can be understood.

Putting these points together you can see the problem that was presented to the union a few years ago. Quite rightly, as union members pay contributions to their union for us to look after their interests, they were saying to us 'What are you going do do about it? How can you assist with the problems that have been created by these changes?' We wanted to do something positive and constructive. There was certainly an element in our thinking at the time which said that perhaps unions were too good at getting on the television and telling everybody what is wrong with everything. When the question was asked of them: 'What are you doing about this problem yourself?' unions did not have too much to say. We wanted to avoid that type of criticism: we wanted to present people with what we thought was a very real problem, and then say that people could come and see what we were doing ourselves.

We came to the conclusion in 1979 that we should move into technical training ourselves. At the time I was a negotiating official at the union based in the South East, and all we did at first was to hire in some equipment. We were fortunate in that we already had two residential training colleges at the time, in Esher and Cudham, we could use as a base. We just hired equipment and ran 1-week courses. What amazed us was that the courses were not only extremely popular with our members, but with employers as well.

To cut a long story short, the whole thing has developed since then as we have never been able to keep up with the demand for our training. We now have about 13 lecturing staff plus technician support staff. We have the two residential colleges, and ten regional training centres in Motherwell, Newcastle, Stockton, Wakefield, Manchester, Birmingham, Nottingham, Bristol, Swansea, and Southport. We have now also reached the point where we can offer the training in-plant on employers' premises as another option. I think that this is one of the important reasons why the training that we have done has been successful: we have made it as flexible as we can in the way in which we offer it. All the training is in units of 1 week because that is a good time for people being released: if you talk about people being released for longer than that you start to run into problems. We can offer courses on a residential basis, in our own training centres, or in-plant; in each case we have tried to keep the training as practically orientated as possible.

We have never found that our members are against this development. On the contrary, they do not seem to be able to get enough of it. It is a unique activity for a union to be involved in, and when we started nobody in our union could forsee the part that it could play in our union. Quite honestly some thought that it was not the sort of thing that a union should get involved in. We have had the full support of our members and of the employers: over 800 companies have used us so far which has been a resounding success as far as the union is concerned.

Recently, we have also developed a distance learning programme, so that people can study the subjects comprising the new technology at home, backed up by 1-day tutorial schools. Another recent development has been an interactive video programme that we have developed with some financial help from the Department of Trade and Industry. We use a video disc system based on a Philips laser disc controlled by a computer, which is itself a very up to date training system. An individual can sit in front of that system: it is an interactive system so he can get the information from it, he can put information into it, he can work at his own pace and in his own time. It is particularly important to the older fellows that we have along to our training centre. They can afford to make themselves look daft without feeling the consequences of it. It is an important consideration that a lot of people sitting with a group of other students will not ask the questions they want to ask or develop the things they want to develop because they feel that they may be making themselves look Charlies at the end of it.

We have seen a number of effects of these problems and the positive approach taken by our union. One is the effect on the grading of what we generally call the common craft rate in industry. There is a concept that a craftsman is a craftsman is a craftsman. It is still a theme which holds in most of industry, but it is coming under increasing strain because of the impact of technology. It deserves the attention of both employers and unions in terms of trying to resolve the problem of accommodating people who see their skills have been dramatically and radically altered over a fairly short period of time. The change of skill level, if that is the right way to put it, is also reflected in the apprenticeship pattern. In our own union, 3 years ago, I did a survey of a thousand of our apprentices, and over 60 per cent were doing technician studies at college, not craft studies. I suspect that the figure is at least as much as 85 per cent now. This means that the change that I am talking about in adult grading structures is mirrored at apprenticeship level, certainly as far as our union is concerned. Of course, we as a union have to accommodate this new type of worker as well as our more traditional workers.

The last issue which I want to touch on I have referred to earlier: multi-skilling or job flexibility. In purely technical terms, I can see the logic of multi-skilling. We have at our training centre a complete robotic centre that employs two industrial robots. There are three computers supporting it. There are various programs that the computers use: interfacing to electronics, pneumatics, hydraulics, and so on. For anyone to really understand that system they have to understand it as a fully integrated system. It is very difficult and I appreciate this point for an individual to say 'I am the electrician; I am just going to look after the electrics on this' or 'I am the fitter; I am just going to look after the moving parts'. I think that, first of all, we must acknowledge the logic of the technological argument concerning multi-skilling, but again we must note the changes in attitudes that are also required of people at all levels of work if we are to cope with these massive changes that are being thrust upon us at the moment, and they are as important as the technological drive.

Multi-skilling is a particular subject in itself. It is not an issue which we would raise with an employer: it is highly improbable that you would find us suggesting striking a multi-skilling deal with a company or another union. In reality, however, we know that companies are increasingly seeking to discuss such matters. Companies are coming to us and stating their requirements. They see it as an important development for the future which must be discussed. Under these circumstances we feel that it is not something that we can turn our backs on. We are prepared to discuss multi-skilling as an issue when it is raised in that fashion, both with companies and with other unions. It is not an issue that you could treat in isolation from any other group within the work force.

We do not want an unconditional discussion. All too often companies come to us with one piece of A4 paper with six points written on it, saying, 'This is what we want out of multi-skilling, and by the way can we have it from the first of December this year, and we want total flexibility across the board'. That seems ridiculous, but it is what is happening. Companies are trying to change traditional working practices that have been with us for decades, very often on their own insistence, and they are trying to change them overnight. That is not on. It is not a thing which we are prepared to do, and I am sure that the AEU are not prepared to do it either.

If we enter discussions on multi-skilling, we want to know that there is some pattern of reward for additional skills gained. We will want to know if there is a job evaluation basis for the wage structure in existence and, if so, whether that structure can cope with the new changes. If there is a financial incentive scheme in operation, we will need to know how that is to be affected by new proposals. Will there be protection of earnings during and subsequent to any retraining? Will new grades have to be created? We will want to know what savings or improvements in a company's fortunes could result from agreements on multi-skilling. For example, would the quality of the product improve? Are there any reductions in scrap and reworking? Will machines of increased speed be employed and, if they are, will output be increased? What savings in materials can be expected? Will there be a more economic use of materials? What will happen to overall production costs and why? Will efficiency improve? If manpower reductions are unavoidable, what savings will accrue?

Our basic position is that the sort of change we are talking about should not result in a redundancies programme. Our fear is that a lot of organizations will see multi-skilling as a means to bring about a major rationalization, a re-working in particular of the maintenance workforce. That again is not on as far as we are concerned. We would like to know whether there will be any changes to existing hours of work. Will shift-work be affected in any way? Will you have to have a call-out system? From our point of view, the issue of multi-skilling is a very large one. It is being raised with us, it is not one we can accept unconditionally, and it is not the sort of change we could envisage bringing in overnight.

Our experience of agreements over new technology indicates that it is usually a long hard slog, and you get there very slowly, but I do believe that you can get there in the end.

6   The management of Advanced Information Technology

IGOR ALEKSANDER

Advanced Information Technology is at its best when it makes us think about how we conduct our affairs. There are elements of AIT which both aid and obstruct this, and my purpose here is to look at some of them.

The caution of Sir Geoffrey Allen over what can reasonably be expected from AIT is reassuring. One needs to be realistic and sceptical about some of the advances that are being talked of. Derek Seddon is, of course, correct in pointing out the interest of computer modelling, but interesting as undoubtedly it is, we need a little more to save the British economy. Our economy is in a mess for the reason that the market share of most British manufacturers, taking the whole lot together, is sliding on the world scale, including home markets. This is the main cause of unemployment and so far no one has found a way of getting a grip on it. Productivity figures are meaningless because a firm can be at its most productive the day before closure.

Derek Barker has already provided some sobering thoughts on the operation of IT solutions and I wish to return to what he has said. I note that John Taylor is more optimistic about knowledge based systems, but I am very interested in the issue of training raised by Bill Jordan and Dave Rogers. Training and re-training would seem to be the crucial consideration for a society in the throes of rapid technological change.

Advanced Information Technology is an uncomfortable term. Nothing can be said to be advanced when one knows that something is bound to be more advanced tomorrow. Its only advantage as a label for what is happening today is that it does give the impression of a dynamic field of activity. It reminds us that change is rapidly taking place and that we have to adapt to a changing situation. So advancing information technology is at its most effective when we are compelled to think about the ways in which we live and work. What one needs to ensure is that one remains unconfused.

The management of AIT is critical. At the Kobler Unit for IT Management we have become increasingly aware of the impact its introduction can have on companies and organizations. I would argue that new technology in itself cannot make UK industry more effective, and though it can provide tools for people to use, there is a very real danger in regarding AIT or IT as a general panacea. This, then, is my conclusion, which I shall now try to justify.

When I was first appointed to the chair of the Management of Information Technology, I consulted the Oxford Dictionary in order to discover what the word 'manage' actually means. According to this reference work, it means to handle, wield, conduct, and control, so that I conclude the management of IT is the handling, wielding, conducting and controlling of IT. This still seems reasonable to me. The word 'management' is more troublesome because the Oxford Dictionary does not give the meaning commonly used. One of its definitions even implies the notion of contrivance, deceit, and trickery. I suppose one could say that management of IT is the deployment of new technology for increased benefits, but this still seems too narrow an idea. The more I ponder the question the more I am inclined to suggest as a progressive definition:

Management of AIT

Narrow: Think again about management
Broad: Think again about AIT
Broader: Think again

Even the definition of Advanced Information Technology ought to encourage reflection when one recalls that its field of activities includes desk-top computers, workstations on a network, robot control, cable television, and other forms of communication. It is salutory to note that the lustre attaching to several of these has dimmed since 1982.

The Alvey view of AIT is also less attractive today. When the report was being written, very powerful people around the Cambridge area convinced John Alvey that knowledge-based machinery was the way to go. So does one simply rewrite the previous list like this?

desk-top computer and knowledge base;
workstation on a network and knowledge base;

robot control and knowledge base;
anything and knowledge base;

Personally, I do not think so. My own definition turns on usability and the number of people who can use the technology to some purpose. Put in this way, AIT should be measured as follows:

Not advanced = not usable
Advancement = usability (according to the number of people who use it)

Usability and benefit and the assessment of benefit are the key issues.

The most obvious pay-off from advancing technology can be seen amongst manufacturers at the operations level, as in, say, a fast working calculating program involved with a flexible manufacturing system. The advance brought about by a robot is obvious; things move fast and continuously, the automation providing a visible pay-off. Computer-aided design is another easily identified activity. Big engineering firms are doing well because they have started using computer-aided design in order to avoid a lot of tentative metal cutting. This technology allows a company to get a long way down the production process without costly mistakes.

Why then is it so difficult to add a knowledge base here? Because it really is. One current grant at the Kobler Unit is concerned with the design of aircraft undercarriages. We have started to consider how we might encompass the knowledge possessed by a designer of aircraft undercarriages so as to turn this information into an Expert System. We have ended up playing around with little blocks of wood, trying to decide how one puts one block of wood on top of another block of wood in a computer. This only goes to show how design is one of the great mysteries in engineering. People are incapable of explaining what they do and few attempts at eliciting knowledge have so far proved successful. I labour the point because one must distinguish between those things that are available to knowledge bases and those things that are not.

Knowledge-based workstations are obviously desirable but they are not here yet. In this context, the Alvey clubs in business are worth watching.

Seven or eight clubs have been set up by the Alvey/KBS director-ate and they are attempting to assess the value of knowledge-based systems. They are in the business of assessment, however informally they may proceed. They are saying 'This is useful' or 'That isn't'. They are not pursuing things which in their view are unhelpful. Such an approach is valuable: there is a need to assess things properly, even in the face of the fact that the assessment involved in the introduction of any form of technology is very difficult, as these examples illustrate.

The first example is the common one: 'It's indispensable, that's why I want it'. Usually, this justification is given by keen managers (often in the United States), without any real attention being paid to the usefulness of the newly introduced technology. 'We certainly couldn't do without it' is often the clinching argument. How inaccurate this perception may be can be demonstrated by the following example.

A law firm consists of three partners and two secretaries. The finances work out as follows:

Turnover	£150 000	
Costs	£50 000	3 × 25 000 (partners)
Salaries	£100 000	2 × 12 250 (secretaries)
Cost of five workstations	£20 000	

This small law firm distributes salaries according to turnover. The idea of introducing new technology arises. In order not to depress the living standards of anyone working in the firm, however, a bank loan is needed for the five workstations chosen, with say a repayment of £8000 over 4 years. The point to notice is that there has to be an increase in turnover of something just over 5 per cent, if the bank loan is to be paid on schedule. Why purchase the workstations at all? How can one be certain that their use will result in the needed increase of turnover? There can be no certainty here. It is impossible *in advance* to assert that workstations are indispensable.

A second example, equally inappropriate, but nastier, turns on the argument which says 'let us replace human beings by machines'. In the early 1980s the principle idea was that secretaries were about to be eliminated from most offices by word processors. Now it is recognized that a word processor does not replace a secretary, although its use in an office may well alter her duties and the pattern of her work.

The 'let's replace human beings by machines' strategy applied to the same law firm commences with the sacking of one of the secretaries, the saving on her salary being set against the four workstations now required.

Costs   £50 000
Loan   £6 000
Salaries £87 500
Total   £143 500

To finance this new technology an annual turnover of £143 500 is necessary. The question is, having lost a member of staff, will the firm be able to maintain this turnover? It is also quite likely that the sacked secretary was doing something valuable, so that the chance of reaching this amount would be slim.

Here we have one of the most important factors in the assessment of IT. Managers have to assess the added value that the introduction of machinery will bring to what people are already doing. The pay-off is in terms of the value added to people. At the moment, Paul Strassmann, ex-vice president of Xerox and visiting Professor in the Kobler Unit, is developing a new economic method based on the value added by people, on the returns one obtains in employing people rather than on capital. I fully expect that this new formulation will, in time, have an enormous effect on the way Western economies are managed.

So, the third example adopts this approach. It considers how the introduction of new technology will enhance turnover by reallocating work in such a manner that the value of what people do will be greater. Closer analysis of the activities of the partners reveals that one spends time on accounts, another on VAT returns. Given suitable software packages, these duties can be passed to a secretary with a new workstation, leaving the two partners more time for legal practice. The result is bound to be increased turnover, which means that such a carefully thought out approach to the introduction of new technology will more than pay for itself. An interesting spin-off here is the upskilling and increase of responsibility of the secretary concerned. Many commentators have wrongly assumed that IT usually causes deskilling.

Currently, several studies show the eventual performance of companies that have moved into IT. In a nutshell, the findings indicate that 50 per cent of the firms improve their performance, while 50 per cent perform worse than before—and this is the same across the developed world. In Britain, very few examples of improved performance exist. Where improvement generally occurs is where significant upskilling results from the introduction of new technology, a fact which brings me to the first commandment of IT management:

> The purchase of IT will pay off only
> if it is driven by a redistribution of
> tasks such that professional skills
> are better used

Where would knowledge bases fit into this scenario? Quite well on reflection, for the reason that knowledge bases have the potential of transmitting the skills of a professional to the someone less qualified. An Expert System is simply a way of encompassing things that may be useful to a person who is trying to acquire more knowledge. At present the Manpower Services Commission has cottoned on to this notion in the field of training and retraining. Providing its funds are spent with the 'First Commandment of IT Management' in mind, then there is a chance of upskilling people. However, once again it is imperative that we be careful over hype. There are things eminently suited to knowledge bases—legislation, fault diagnosis, and technical procedures—but anything that necessitates judgemental knowledge cannot be sensibly included. Simulations of judgement must never be allowed to disguise the superficial nature of the decisions being suggested. No hospital can replace doctors with Expert Systems.

Because Expert Systems are not advanced enough to hold judgemental knowledge, the deliberately cautious approach of the Alvey business clubs is to be commended. Hype is everywhere in IT, but especially in AIT. Too many pundits today are still prepared to propose that new technology is endowed with exaggerated and unproven properties. Almost characteristic of Artificial Intelligence, hype has now unfortunately attached itself to Expert Systems. Take for instance this 1959 pronouncement:

In the visible future AI research will produce computers with problem-solving powers co-extensive with the range to which the human mind has been applied (Simon and Newell 1972).

The visible future? One could be kind I suppose and say the visible future is the year 2000. Even then, a prediction of this kind does not seem reasonable. As new systems are developed, its grandiose target of competence appears less and less practicable. Worst of all the pundits is undoubtedly Marvin Minsky, the grand-daddy of hype at MIT. In 1980 he said:

In from 3 to 8 years we will have a machine with the general intelligence of an average human being. I mean a machine that will be able to read Shakespeare, grease a car, play office politics, tell a joke, have a fight. At that point, the machine will be able to educate itself with a fantastic speed. In a few months, it will be at genius level, and a few months after that its power will be incalculable.

What is worrying about such a blatant oversimplification of the development problems involved in AI research is that Minsky is a bright guy. Why then does he feel compelled to say these patent untruths? Why should his utterance be so unconstrained?

Consider the claim Minsky dared to make as recently as 6 years ago. The machine he predicted would be able to read. That is not unreasonable, if one means that it is able to translate words into ASC II characters. However, if one asked the machine to paraphrase what it had read, then this is something beyond its capabilities. Read Shakespeare, turn Shakespeare into ASC II characters certainly, but comprehend Shakespeare, no way at all. Of course, a robot can grease a car, but the idea that greasing cars and office politics are in the same performance range is absurd, misleading, and dangerous. Telling a joke is certainly the most unlikely activity of all. Good jokes require a profound understanding of the nature of the human condition. How can this subtle awareness be readily given to a machine?

Computer-generated stories alone should remind us how complicated the processes of creative writing actually are. The ones I have read verge on the idiotic. They include such literary bombshells as 'Fred was walking along the river bank. He fell in'. Although more sophisticated examples may be found I find it remarkable that any such computer-generated prose should have impressed anybody. It could hardly compete with the first beginnings of composition in a primary school classroom. To suggest that the two sentences reveal any real grasp of the world is naive.

It is only under sceptical pressure, say, with respect to machine translation, that workers in AI begin to admit their failings and we begin to perceive the inevitable limitations of new technology, now and in the foreseeable future.

I suppose the crux of the AI problem over hype is that the experts themselves are invariably locked into selling. In order to attract research funds, they have tended to extrapolate and predict astonishing computer possibilities—for the benefit of the media. Mike Bywater, in *The Observer*, has suggested that this kind of hype arose from the need to impress the US Defence Department. He wrote: 'Artificial Intelligence is a two-word phrase which makes US Department of Defence Officials salivate when they hear it'. My own view is slightly different. A prime source of exaggeration I believe is an inability amongst computer scientists to consider the limitations of what they are doing. Because it is so easy to signal progress by multiplying existing accomplishments into future possibilities, there has been an absence of critical awareness, of any acceptance of failure, in most professional discussions of Artificial Intelligence. A cynic might comment that it is not profitable to talk of shortcomings. Hypes are attention-catching and offer swift returns. Obviously there are horrendous dangers in these sorts of exaggeration when they beguile defence establishments. It could be termed the SDI effect.

An imaginary dialogue between a top computer scientist and the president of a major power might go like this.

Computer Scientist: 'AIT can do anything'.

President: 'We shall deploy AIT to provide a shield over our country, since AIT can do anything'.

Computer Scientist: 'Mr President, our computers are not quite ready to do that yet'.

President: 'I will not listen to subversive Anti-American Computer Scientists'.

Strategic Advisor: 'Mr President, with SDI we can win a nuclear war'.

An ageing movie star: 'It's High Noon for me. I'll show that SOAB. Where's my gun—I mean the button'.

Surely, the worry here is the very idea that Artificial Intelligence is omnipotent. That is why I have so little sympathy with computer scientists who are upset by the application of AI research to the Strategic Defence Initiative, not because they think it is bound to fail, but for the reason that they think it might work. They, too, are guilty of believing AIT can do everything asked of it.

Hence, my 'Second Commandment of IT Management', which runs

Both makers and users of advancing
information technology are under

obligation to quote the limitations of
their work whenever they quote its potential

The obligation to be self-aware in AIT is unavoidable. One must be willing to acknowledge limitations as well as advances. The following limitations of AIT are necessary

(1)   Artificial intelligence in computers only mimics the superficial informational behaviour of human beings. It neither provides an explanation of the mechanism of thought nor achieves a performance comparable to the human brain.

(2)   Knowledge engineering is only the storage of a highly specialized class of knowledge that is *elicitable*. Most human knowledge is not of this kind.

(3)   Expert Systems can no more replace an expert than the AA guide to trouble-shooting replaces a mechanic.

If we accept that these are the limitations of AIT, what responsibilities do educators have? For a start, they need to make sense of 'computer literacy', a grotesque term for anything to do with computers.

Computer literacy has properly nothing to do with programming, even in PROLOG. Programming is nothing more than the result of the failure of computers to be usable. I can recall days when colleagues would mention that a new computer language called BASIC was totally interactive, absolutely wonderful, and immediately accessible. Now I notice others wave banners saying 'BASIC is bad for health'. PASCAL, MODULA2, ADA, PROLOG, HOPE— the computer languages we have praised, then reassessed.

What then does computer literacy mean? It means knowing and approaching scientifically the limitations of computers; it means putting new technology in perspective. There can be no excuse for ignorance on the grounds that technological change is too rapid to allow a considered view. Companies who embrace AIT simply because their competitors have done so are doomed to fail. One cannot afford to introduce computers without thinking through what they are expected to accomplish. In other words, technological change must only be used to allow people to do what they have always wanted to do. As I reflected earlier, a part of our national problem is that many managers do not know what they want to do.

Management decisions can never afford to depend on 'let's go and see what IT is available and then think how we might use it'. The only safe starting-point for the introduction of new technology in any organization must always be a statement of objectives. Until this is crystal clear, it is impossible to know whether microelectronic tools will be of any help at all. Human beings should never forget what they are good at doing; their strength will always reside in grasping what is at stake. That is why the success of the management of IT relies on a human appreciation of the needs to be addressed.

Appendix: the Bide Report

Advanced research work has become concentrated in research centres and institutes, where the necessary hardware, software, and technical expertise can be brought together. It has become apparent that only limited results can be expected from individuals working alone, and that collaboration is essential both at the research and the development stages.

The Alvey Programme (from 1983 onwards)

A major impetus to the development of collaborative research was given by the Japanese Fifth Generation Research Project, drawing together the eight leading Japanese electronics companies with the Ministry of International Trade and Industry, following an international survey of research in Advanced Information Technology. Overseas governments and research groups were invited to join the programme in 1981. In the United Kingdom a committee was set up in 1982, chaired by John Alvey of British Telecom, and with Brian Oakley as secretary, to advise the government on appropriate response. Their report (the Alvey report) made positive recommendations:

We have concluded not merely that there is scope in the UK for collaborative research but that such collaborative endeavours are essential if we are to preserve and strengthen our competitiveness in IT.

The Alvey Committee concluded that although there were very few experienced practitioners of Advanced Information Technology in the United Kingdom, a broad community wished to be able to benefit from their work:

There is a solid consensus amongst industrialists and among the many other knowledgeable people in the IT community whom we have consulted that the areas which we have identified are key to the future development of IT. There is a general agreement on the priorities which need to be tackled in these sectors.

The technical priority areas were Intelligent Knowledge Based Systems (applications of Artificial Intelligence), Software Engineering, Man–Machine Interface, and Very Large Scale Integration. In addition, large demonstrator projects required technologies from each of the priority areas, and a Parallel Declarative Systems Architecture programme sought to provide a strong technical basis for the new generation of computer systems. Central to the success of the programme would be novel forms of collaboration, themselves an experiment:

The programme should be a collaborative effort between industry, the academic sector and other research organisations, in order to improve the harnessing of our technical strengths to industrial objectives; to get the best value from Government support; and to allow the widest possible involvement and exploitation.

During the same period discussions in the European Community led to the establishment of the ESPRIT Programme for collaborative work in the same field, requiring unprecedented degrees of collaboration between individuals and institutions in Community countries, and a close relationship with the Alvey programme.

The Bide Report (December 1986)

The Alvey programme was established in 1983, with financial support from government and industry for a collaborative programme costing a total of £350 million, lasting until 1988–1989. By the beginning of 1986 the full budget of the programme was committed to collaborative projects, and a further committee was established, chaired by Sir Austin Bide of Glaxo, to make recommendations for future activities. Their report was submitted in November 1986, and sought to build on the experience of the Alvey Programme.

The Alvey programme aimed to provide an initiative leading to greater competitiveness in IT suppliers. As the programme was conceived to develop the longer term technologies to meet that objective in the 1990s, it is too soon to comment on its specific technical achievement. However, there is no doubt, from the evidence which we have received, that Alvey has been successful in drawing together industry and universities in a much closer relationship than was previously the case, and has stimulated collaboration between companies normally in competition to attack common research problems. The result is that there is already a much stronger research base from which UK industry can and should now go forward to develop competitive IT applications. More, however, needs to be done.

Given the relatively adolescent stage of research in Advanced Information Technology, and the small scale of successful British commercial exploitation of the technology to date, considerable further research and development is clearly needed. The Bide Committee was largely concerned with the development and exploitation phases, and largely made up of Information Technology supplier and user companies, with only three professors speaking for university academic research. Companies represented on the main committee include GEC, Plessey, British Telecom, Thorn–EMI, STC, ICL, Systems Designers, Racal, Sainsbury, PACTEL, Barclays Bank, Ferranti, and British Aerospace.

They were particularly concerned with financial aspects of the field, noting the damaging effects of short-term thinking in companies and financial organizations:

High interest rates and the short term outlook of financial organisations in the UK do not encourage a high rate of investment by UK industry in long term research and development, and in the promotion of entrepreneurial marketing strategies, except in market niches.

Attention was given to the issue of the stage at which competitive profit mechanisms should intervene:

'How far does the collaborative process go?' is a question that requires an answer.

Financial interests and financial risk were given more attention than research interest, and academic inquiry and speculation, which were assumed to be catered for elsewhere and unspecified:

There is ... a mutual interest between IT users and suppliers which we believe can and should be developed further. A purposeful collaborative programme developing specific applications of IT would not only contribute to the competitiveness of the users involved but also let suppliers demonstrate products with which they intend to seek world markets. Government assistance can reduce the risk which stands in the way of such projects and increase the priority that participants give to them.

Collaboration, not only between users and suppliers but also between IT users themselves, is critical, since it enables them to share the growing cost and complexity of IT systems development. Groups of users who normally compete with each other may have a common interest in a sub-system capability (for example, standard coding of merchandise). Groups of dissimilar users can collectively be made more efficient through the use of a common system (for example, electronic funds transfer).

Whilst we recognise that an academic research programme must, at least in part, be free to follow interesting lines of enquiry, virtually all research involving the participation of industry will be directed towards recognised product goals.

It is instructive to see how the field of Intelligent Knowledge Based Systems is described by such a group after the involvement of their institutions in collaborative research in the field. Their report seeks to identify a consensus view:

5.17 The term 'Intelligent Knowledge Based Systems' includes autonomous systems such as robots, and interactive systems which provide human users with suitably tailored decisions, diagnoses, advice and personal tuition. Ever increasing complexity provokes a need for new design tools, new system building tools and more intelligent user interfaces. To provide computing power to support these complex systems, coarse grain parallel computing engines are required. System building tools based on logic are seen as the bridge between the low level systems architecture and high level IKBS formalisms.

5.18 IKBS is a generic term, encompassing expert systems for diagnostic, signal interpretation and design tasks; intelligent front ends to simplify interaction with complicated application programs; planning/scheduling systems for non-linear tasks, and intelligent tutoring systems. Further research is necessary into the development of new high level tools for representing and manipulating functional, causal and temporal relationships, for the support of non-monotonic reasoning and for knowledge fusion. This should be combined with pull-through of the powerful second generation 'system shells' for expert systems, planning systems and intelligent front ends, under development in the current Alvey IKBS programme.

5.19 To make interactive systems more sensitive to human users, there is a need for further research into powerful computational mechanisms for generating appropriate responses. Issues include content, form and control of information feedback. In particular, there is an urgent requirement to develop computational techniques for representing a user's knowledge, goals and intentions.

5.20 Communication in unrestricted natural language would significantly ease the problem of man–machine communication (as distinct from man–machine interaction). This includes both interpretation and generation systems. Research topics include logical and computational properties of meaning representations, theories of discourse, computational grammars and generation models. Further research is required, coupled with pull-through of tools and systems architecture, under development now.

5.21 The goals here are the development of more formalisms, based upon logic, and the design and implementation of new logic-based systems building tools to bridge between these high level formalisms and the new systems architectures, particularly parallel architectures. This is a significant activity within the existing Alvey IKBS programme which will yield many exploitable tools. But there are questions to be answered about the nature of the mapping between the problem solving architectures of complex knowledge based tasks and processing and memory parallelisms.

Experience of managed collaborative research has suggested that a degree of direction is required, though individual researchers are likely to be unhappy with the sweeping suggestion for removal of funding, as many current key technologies, such as logic programming and theorem proving, have been previously classified as cul de sacs in the United States.

It must be a prime objective in prosecution of the Research Effort, as in the completion of Alvey, to ensure that those technologies which show most promise continue to evolve and that support is removed from those which lead to blind alleys.

It is emphasized that the continuation of research, development, and application of advanced training information technology depends on new measures in education and training. Section 6 of the report deals with Education and Training:

6.1 Suppliers and users of IT based systems are unanimous in their concern about the shortage of those with the IT skills they need. In the survey conducted jointly in June 1986 by the national Computer Centre and IT Skills Agency more than 20% of IT users and more than 25% of software suppliers stated that they were 'crippled' or have their 'survival threatened' by shortages of skilled staff.

6.2 The situation is thus apparently much as it was when the Butcher Committee reported (in 1984) that 'the market could comfortably absorb more graduates with the requisite skills', despite the very considerable expansion of training opportunities at all levels that has occurred since then. ... Significantly arts and humanities students were as successful as scientists and engineers in finding IT employment after taking such conversion courses, although the actual jobs they did were often quite different.

6.3 By no means all shortages are at specialist graduate level. Many of the tasks required from IT users can be carried out effectively by people with a less advanced academic background, trained in their own homes or at local centres with the aid of relatively modest interactive facilities and centrally generated course material. Investment by the nation in training of this type would be amply justified not only by its benefit to the IT industry but also as a means of enhancing the employment prospects of less qualified people.

6.4 Paradoxically, companies are often reluctant to expand their in-house training programmes. In its 1986 report 'A Call to Action' the Engineering Council stated that 'the most common reason given for unwillingness to invest in continuing education and training was poaching. Poaching was considered to be more economic and, in some cases, more desirable and convenient . . .'

6.5 One of the specimen application projects we have developed—Distance Learning for Senior Management—is a project to educate and inform senior management in the UK economy at large on the potential of IT to transform their business and stimulate new opportunities. The project seeks to highlight the way in which IT can help solve geography and time constraints on business activities as well as explain IT's well established role in fast and efficient information processing.

6.6 The very success of the Alvey programme adds to the skill shortage problem. Very skilled (and scarce) talents are needed for the programme itself and as the user community begins to take up the resulting products, the demands of users for skilled staff are bound to increase both quantitatively and qualitatively. In the long run, the kind of innovations pioneered by the Alvey programme should lead to more 'user friendly' systems (i.e. systems which can be used by non-specialists). . . .

6.7 We believe that the situation is such that it demands an imaginative response from Government and industry alike. . . .

6.8 However even the most skilled staff need not necessarily come from courses of the existing type. The specific needs of the IT suppliers organisations and their customers are likely to diverge as the products of the Alvey programme enter widespread use. Many user organisations now feel that existing computer science based courses, at all levels, are inappropriate to the needs of their staff.

6.9 There is a clear need for courses which bring together IT and business skills. . . .

6.10 We also recommend that encouragement should be given to the further development of interactive distance learning techniques, (i.e. techniques which allow the student to react, through a video display, to the course material) aimed at training people with a less developed academic background to qualify for employment in the user industries.

6.11 In making our proposals we are conscious that, too frequently, the responsibility for implementing recommendations such as these lie with no particular body. We believe that it is important that the management arrangements for any new initiative include a responsibility for education and training. The collaborative culture, both between individual companies and companies and academia, should relate to education and training as well as to research.

References

Alvey Committee. (1982). *Advanced Information Technology*. HMSO, London.

Barnett, C. (1986). *The Audit of War*. Macmillan.

Bide Committee. (1986). *Information Technology: The National Resource*. HMSO, London.

Cabinet Office Paper. (1986). *Learning to Live with IT: An Overview of the Potential of Information Technology for Education and Training*, Information Technology Advisory Panel. HMSO, London.

Ennals, R. and Cotterell, A. (1985). *Fifth Generation Computers: Their Implications for Further Education*, FEU Occasional Paper. DES.

Handy, C. and Aitken, R. (1986). *Understanding Schools as Organisations*. Pelican.

Minsky, M. (ed.) (1968). *Semantic Information Processing*. MIT Press.

Simon, H. and Newell, A. (1972). *Human Problem Solving*. Prentice-Hall.

Tompsett, C. (1986). 'Information Technology: The Fifth General and FE'. *Education*, 17 January, 1986.